THE GREAT WHITE TENT

Published by: Evangelical Contribution On Northern Ireland
12 Wellington Place, Belfast BT1 6GE

Cover Design By: Spring Graphics

Printed by: GPS Colour Graphics Ltd.

ISBN 1 874324 46 8

ECONI 1999

THE GREAT WHITE TENT

edited by Alwyn Thomson

CONTENTS

FOREWORD

David McMillan

THE PUBLICATION OF THIS BOOK PRESENTS A HUGE CHALLENGE TO THE Protestant community in Northern Ireland and to the evangelical community in particular.

Protestant culture, and the evangelical sub-culture that is a part of it, not only seeks to define its own story for and by itself but seeks also to define, with certainty and authority, those outside its boundaries and its opponents. Furthermore, because of the assumed religious, philosophical and moral superiority of our own culture or sub-culture the voices and opinions of the outsider or opponent are prejudged as of little worth or, indeed, so corrupt as to be positively dangerous if heeded or taken seriously.

As far as evangelicals are concerned, the voice that speaks the truth to any society or community about its true nature is the Bible - authoritative, divinely inspired and true. Yet, as John Stott has argued so persuasively, to hear what the Bible is saying requires a process of double listening.

We must listen to the Bible and listen to the world. Then we must apply the message of the Bible in a relevant and meaningful way to the real world in which we live, not the closeted world of our sub-cultures. Living in a divided community such as Northern Ireland demands the faithful application of that principle of double listening.

This book presents a challenge to members of the Protestant community generally and the evangelical community in particular. The challenge is to be prepared to listen to the opinions of those whom we lived along side, yet for so long have been strangers to, as they reflect on how we appear to them.

The fearful aspect of this challenge for evangelicals is not that we will be forced to change our understanding of the gospel. Rather, it is that we may find that our presentation of the gospel in life and in word has been seriously compromised by our commitment to, or ambivalence towards, cultural and political mantras such as *For God and Ulster*.

The positive aspect of the challenge is that we may, with God's help and a dose of humility, be better equipped to reflect more faithfully the measure of grace we have met in Christ. As the Scottish bard put it:

> *O wad some Pow'r the giftie gie us*
> *To see oursels as others see us!*
> *It wad frae mony a blunder free us,*
> *And foolish notion.*

INTRODUCTION

Alwyn Thomson

IN **1996 ECONI** PUBLISHED *FAITH IN ULSTER*. THAT BOOK, LIKE THIS one, was part of a wider project, entitled *God, Land and Nation*, that explores the relationship between religious and political identities.

The purpose of *Faith in Ulster* within that wider project was to give an opportunity to a diverse group of individuals from a Protestant or unionist or evangelical background to tell how they see their identity.

Specifically, each contributor to *Faith in Ulster* was asked to respond to the question, What does the phrase *For God and Ulster* mean to you? This phrase, with its historic resonance in the unionist community and its linking of religious and political identities, provided the focus for reflection on unionist identity and the place of Protestantism within that identity.

The response to *Faith in Ulster* from many quarters was very encouraging. Some of those who responded suggested ways in which we could build on the book. We, too, had been considering the options.

Of the many possibilities open to us we decided that we would produce this follow up publication which would give an opportunity to a range of contributors from a Catholic or nationalist tradition to share their perceptions of unionist identity.

Specifically, we asked each contributor to respond to the question, What do you see as the distinctive characteristics of unionist identity? Contributors were also encouraged to comment, where appropriate, on the role they saw religion playing in that identity.

The book has taken longer to produce than originally anticipated. A number of those invited to contribute declined the invitation, being hesitant about addressing such a sensitive issue in a brief piece intended for publication. The wider political background also created some difficulties. Not a few potential contributors were actively involved in negotiating the Agreement and in the subsequent Referendum and Assembly election campaigns. Events over the summer also absorbed a lot of their time and energy.

A number of reviewers of *Faith in Ulster* drew attention to the small number of contributions from women. They will notice a similar patter in this volume. Despite our efforts to ensure a greater representation from women we were unsuccessful. Part of the difficulty arises in that both politics and the church - especially at leadership levels - continue to be male dominated. However, there does seem to be some reluctance on the part of women to address some of these questions or to address them in this kind of way. If this is so an investigation into the reasons why it is so might make an interesting study in its own right. However, that is a question for another time.

Our hope is that many ordinary men and women from within the unionist and Protestant tradition will read this book. We hope, too, that opinion formers - whether politicians, clergy or educators - will also find it of value. Not all of the readers will like all of the contributions, or, for that matter, all of the contributors.

However, we believe that through reading the book some in the unionist community will come to understand better the perceptions of their tradition held by their Catholic and nationalist neighbours. We believe, too, that the diversity of opinion represented in just these few contributions will help break down simplistic and stereotypical perceptions of the 'other' community.

We repeat here what we said in *Faith in Ulster*:

If you find this book useful, helpful, provocative, or of value in any way, please make others aware of it.

If this book has stimulated your thinking, expanded you vision or provoked your wrath please let us know.

Finally, for those of you who can no longer control your curiosity about the title of this book I suggest you turn to Seamus Dunn's contribution on page 43.

Gerry ADAMS

Gerry Adams was born in Belfast in 1948. President of Sinn Fein since 1983, he is currently MP for West Belfast and was elected to the Assembly set up under the Stormont Agreement.

He is the author of a number of books including *Falls Memories* (1982), *Cage Eleven* (1990), *The Street and Other Stories* (1992), *Free Ireland: Towards A Lasting Peace* (1995) and his autobiography, *Before the Dawn* (1996).

And all must need, in tolerance combined,
A steady purpose to achieve, extend
Employment, bodily nurture, peace of mind,
When each may grasp his neighbour's hand as friend

Louis MacNeice

IN HIS OWN WAY, THE POET SUMS UP THE REAL GOAL OF THE PEACE process. His sentiment was echoed by Nelson Mandela and Yitzak Rabin who, in their particular circumstances of conflict, both recognised the centrality of making friends with ones enemy if a lasting peace settlement were to be achieved. Mandela said of de Klerk, "To make peace with an enemy, one must work with that enemy, and that enemy become your partner."

Making peace is also about change. It is about changing the structures in our society which provoked, promoted, and sustained conflict, division and violence.

Clearly, there is a huge gap of distrust between nationalists and republicans on the one hand and unionists on the other. It must be bridged and foundations laid on both sides which allow each of us to move toward the other in a spirit of goodwill and growing trust.

Sinn Fein is an Irish republican party. We seek the unity and independence of Ireland as a sovereign nation. We seek an end to British rule in Ireland and an end to the conflict and divisions which have resulted. We are committed to a new Ireland which recognises, reflects and celebrates the diversity of the Irish people. These democratic goals remain our primary political objectives. We believe that this is a reasonable position to hold, to aspire to and to campaign for politically.

Unionists hold a different position - fair enough. Irish republicans want to make friends with our unionist neighbours. We want to put division and fear and violence behind us forever. Our vision of the future is firmly rooted in a view of this island which envisions a unity of people, an inclusiveness in which citizens share on the basis of equality.

The republican philosophy of 200 years ago had as its aim the creation of a socially progressive, tolerant and just society. That remains our aim. Republicans have no wish to discriminate against unionists, to dominate or marginalise unionists, or to treat them as second class citizens. That is the road to more conflict.

As Irish republicans we have tried to reach out to our unionist neighbours. For many reasons that has not always been successful. We have also tried to understand and to analyse the conflict in order to find new ways of engaging with unionism.

It is often said that there are two traditions, or two cultures, in Ireland. In my view there are not. There are scores of traditions, maybe hundreds - female and male, urban and rural, small town and hill village, fishing port and island, inner city and farming community, labourer and artisan, literary and oral, orange and green, protestant and catholic, pagan and Christian, Jew and Muslim and more. All are equally valid, all part of what we are. Together they make up a diverse and rich culture. The sum total of all of this and all that it represents is part of the diversity of the people of this island.

In my view the siege of Derry, like the Battle of the Boyne, is as much an influence and a part of our history as is the siege of Limerick, the Famine or the Easter Rising. The challenge facing us is to take that history, to learn from it and to move forward together. Critical to our success will be the creation of a new relationship based on equality of opportunity and parity of esteem, a relationship in which, when making claims and demands, we seek to take into account the views and opinions of others. There is a common need to recognise the integrity of the other, to be at peace with each other, to understand the way we have hurt one another, to listen to one another and to be patient with one another. In essence we need a partnership.

Shimon Peres said of the Palestine/Israel conflict, "I think what is really important for a peace process is the creation of a partner, more than a plan. Because plans don't create partners, but if you have a partner then you can negotiate a plan."

We need partners for peace who will help us in partnership achieve a lasting settlement. Such partnerships offer an opportunity to tackle shared concerns by concentrating on the responsibilities which we each have. A partnership is about recognising and respecting our differences and accommodating these in a positive and constructive way. It is, by definition, a two way street. It means developing clear, achievable goals and developing and setting criteria and structures capable of bringing visible and durable change. It requires dialogue and mutual support. It requires that people have ownership of this. It has to be about people from very different positions, with different perspectives, goals and objectives, sitting down around the table and seeking to find common positions.

That requires risk taking. But in the first instance it requires a dialogue out of which trust and confidence can grow. My hope is that the unionist leaderships will come to the realisation that talking to republicans makes sense and is their, and our, best way of consolidating the opportunity for peace which now exists and of building a new future for all our people.

Peace is a concern and a responsibility for all of us: citizens, churches, political parties, trade unions, the business community and organisations of every kind. To be durable, peace requires not just the taking of responsibility but the sharing of responsibility and of decision making through a partnership.

In our context that means new ways of thinking and acting. It means reconciliation, it means forgiveness, it means ending the cycle of conflict. Alan Paton, who wrote *Cry the Beloved Country*, one of the most powerful indictments of the apartheid society, said, "There is a hard law...that when a deep injury is done to us, we never recover until we forgive." We must forgive each other. This will be difficult but not impossible. It demands effort and change from all of us. It requires the removal of injustices and inequality. None of this is impossible. If we want it badly enough - and I believe we do - then it is there for the taking.

John
BRUTON

John Bruton was born in Dublin in 1947. He studied economics and politics at UCD and shortly after graduating was elected to the Dail as TD for Meath. He held a number of ministerial posts in Fine Gael governments in the 1980s. He became deputy leader of the party in 1987 and leader in 1990. In 1994 he was elected Taoiseach, a post he held until 1997. Married with four children his publications include *Reform of the Dail* (1980), *A Better Way to Plan the Nation's Finances* (1981) and *Real Issues or Mock Battles* (1986).

I THINK IT IS TRUE THAT A STRONG CHRISTIAN FAITH GIVES PEOPLE SOME sense of their own smallness, some sense of the greater design of the world and, above all, a sense of humility. Without a sense of humility I do not think we would have ethical politics, ethical business or ethical activity of any kind. It is that sense of the transcendental, that sense of something greater than us, that enables us to live a life that is good and true.

I would like to reflect briefly on what the world owes to Irish evangelicals. When you celebrate 300 years of history your celebrations must be of the religious content of your tradition which is, of course, the most important part of it.

But it is important that you should also reflect on the political gift that Irish evangelical churches have given to the world. The democratic character of your churches, right back to their foundations, are a gift to the world. Evangelical churches have been, in many senses, schools of democracy, accountability and equality before the law.

People of the evangelical tradition, who emigrated to America in the seventeenth century, brought ideas of democracy, equality and accountability with them to the New World. These ideas, first brought forward in the context of church governance, were carried into the civil and political sphere and inspired the American Declaration of Independence and Constitution.

The same ideas came back to the old world from America, through France, and inspired the democratisation and republicanisation of Europe during the nineteenth century. But the origin of these ideas lay in the thinking of the small band of emigrants, many of them Ulster-Scots, who set off from Ireland and Britain to the New World during the seventeenth century.

Therefore, I say that those of the Unionist tradition should have nothing to fear from the new structures established under the Good Friday Agreement, based, as they are, on equality between the people they represent and their neighbours. Unionists in Ireland should not feel any sense of 'precarious belonging' or that their place in Ireland is challenged in some way.

Unionists, of course, are not the only ones who feel that way. Nationalists in Northern Ireland feel that their Nationalism, their Irishness, even their Catholicism is, to a degree, challenged by the way in which Northern Ireland operates. Since both communities feel a sense of 'precarious belonging' there is, therefore, a need to build structures which make everybody feel equally at home.

Irish-American author, Padraig O'Malley, who has studied conflict the world over, writing of the Ulster problem said:

Language is central to the lack of understanding between Catholics and Protestants. Nationalist leaders talk about frameworks, while Unionists prefer to deal with definite proposals. The two approaches can be traced back to their theological roots before the Reformation.

In other words, as O'Malley sees it, Protestants take things literally and Catholics think metaphorically. Resultant misunderstandings about the meaning of words and ideas can be fatal to the building of trust. If these differences of language are recognised before the dialogue begins, the difficulties can be overcome.

Some Unionists might regard the new structures established under the Good Friday Agreement as dangerous, viewing them as a provisional arrangement, or a moving staircase, inexorably leading towards something else. Given the existing potential for misunderstanding, there is a great risk in any approach which says, "We'll take half a loaf now and we'll come back in about thirty years for the rest."

The goal of the new structures should be agreement between the two traditions, which both will regard as settling their relationship on a permanent basis. If this is understood, each side should be willing to be generous in its dealings with the other.

There is a place for everybody in Ireland. We all belong here. Ireland belongs in close community with Britain and Europe, with which we have so much in common. There is something British in every Irish person and, to a degree, there is something Irish in every British person, but all of us are Europeans. We share traditions. We are different but we are also, in many senses, the same.

We must find a way of expressing this richness of diversity as something that brings us together, rather than something that divides us. I hope the heritage that past Irish evangelicals have given to world democracy will help present day Irish people of the evangelical tradition to contribute much to the development of democracy, accountability and good government in Ireland, in Britain, in Europe and throughout the world.

Feargal
COCHRANE

Feargal Cochrane was born in Belfast in 1965 and studied in the Department of Politics at Queen's University, Belfast, where he was awarded his PhD in 1992. He was a Research Fellow at the Institute of Irish Studies, QUB in 1993 and was granted an Honorary Fellowship by the Department of Politics, QUB in 1995. His book, *Unionist Politics and the Politics of Unionism since the Anglo-Irish Agreement*, was published in 1997. He was a Research Officer in the Centre for the Study of Conflict at the University of Ulster from 1996-1998. He is currently a lecturer in Politics at the Richardson Institute, University of Lancaster.

BEFORE TAKING A PROFESSIONAL ACADEMIC interest in the unionist community, my conception of unionism as an outsider, was of a group of people determined to dominate the levers of power in Northern Ireland by all means at their disposal, from the constitutional and the democratic, to a resort to civil disobedience and violence when required. As someone who was born and brought up in Belfast, unionism, loyalism and Protestantism were synonymous terms to describe a monolithic and powerful community. More recently, I have come to realise that unionists are a highly complex grouping and that the appearance of power actually belies a deeply felt sense of political and cultural insecurity.

While clearly you do not have to be a Protestant to be a unionist, the culture of protesting is woven into the fabric of the ideology. Unionism by its very nature is a reactive rather than a proactive movement. It is at its strongest and most coherent when it reacts against something that all unionists can commonly agree to be objectionable. For example, Home Rule at the beginning of the century, the ending of Stormont and introduction of direct rule in the 1970s, the Anglo-Irish Agreement in the 1980s and the Framework Document in the 1990s. What these examples all have in common is that they were perceived by unionists as being a threat to their position within the United Kingdom. The trouble starts when unionists have to be more innovative and progressive, when they have to say yes instead of saying no, when they have to decide between various policy options and advocate a united position for moving forward.

One of the central reasons why unionism has difficulty in presenting a positive face to the world emanates from a fear of their political surroundings. This derives from the historical experience of the unionist community. Protestants, after all, were the minority until partition in 1920. The largest group in the north east, the Presbyterians, were regarded as heretics by both the Catholic Church and the dominant Church of Ireland. Unionists had to form a paramilitary army and threaten to rebel against the state to which they professed loyalty in order to avoid being 'sold-out' by the British in 1912. They feared the same was happening in 1973 with the Sunningdale Agreement, in 1985 with the Anglo-Irish Agreement and on several occasions during the 1990s. They have also felt that the Catholic community in the North and the South has wanted to destroy Northern Ireland since its inception; and, technically speaking, the Republic, through Articles 2 & 3 of its Constitution, has been trying to do this since 1937.

In other words, to varying degrees unionists have felt under threat. In practice this has resulted in a feeling that they can trust no-one but themselves, and that at times they cannot even trust each other. This has been very debilitating for the ideology, because if the price of liberty is eternal vigilance, then the price of vigilance is eternal exhaustion, as everyone reads their political tea-leaves for signs of treachery. This has produced an endemic negativism within unionism, where anyone who moves forward in a progressive direction is examined for signs of weakness and undercut if they show any signs of moving away from the status quo. The safest political ground lies, therefore, behind the trenches. Any unionist who moves out from behind the trench risks being sniped at by other unionists motivated either by narrow political opportunism, or by a real fear of betrayal.

One member of the Ulster Unionist Party made the astute observation a few years ago that, "The spirit of Lundyism haunts all within unionism who consider compromise, conciliation or negotiation." I believe that this is a ghost which will have to be exorcised if unionism is to make any progress towards its objective of preserving and strengthening the position of Northern Ireland within the United Kingdom.

The tensions that have ravaged unionism since the signing of the Good Friday Agreement illustrate that ghosts are hard to kill!

Pauline COLL

Pauline Coll was born in mid-Down and educated at Assumption Grammar School, Ballynahinch. She graduated from Queen's University with a degree in Geography and presently teaches in Belfast. Married with 5 children now aged between 13 and 25, she lives in Bangor where she is a member at St Comgall's. She is a former Chairperson and current member of the City of Belfast YMCA Management Board and member of Ploughshare, an inter-denominational community group embracing all traditions.

I CANNOT TELL WHETHER THOSE AMONG WHOM I HAVE LIVED FOR OVER twenty-five years, and with whom I have become friends, vote Unionist or Alliance or for any of the many other parties. Generally, I can say who is Presbyterian or Methodist, Church of Ireland or Baptist or other. I suspect that there are as many shades of unionism as there are theologies in a Catholic congregation! One faith but many theologies!

For almost ten years I have worked closely with yet another group of people who traditionally would not have had any links or association with Roman Catholics. This experience has been a challenge - difficult at times - and ultimately a tremendous enrichment. Over the years we have built a mutual trust, an appreciation of our different emphases and, above all, a shared sense of purpose. This has been hard work, which has not always met with encouragement.

There is considerable suspicion, mistrust and resentment, as much in the Christian church as between political parties. Trust cannot be fabricated. It is an arduous process which involves meeting, getting to know, learning to accept and then building that trust which is the foundation of a shared future.

My understanding of unionist identity is shaped by my personal experiences, together with my own interpretation of unionist politics. The dictionary definition of 'unionist' is, "An opponent of Irish Home Rule," referring to that section of the Liberal Party which opposed Gladstone's Home Rule policy in 1886. It seems, therefore, that unionist identity was primarily founded on opposition and reaction to, and protest against, Home Rule for Ireland. For me, these three words - opposition, reaction, protest - still sum up unionism today, in the general sense.

It is difficult, I think, given the conservative nature of unionism for unionists to countenance political change. Although not all unionists express the same degree of opposition to political change - and some do not express disapproval at all - there is a general discontent, mistrust, sometimes fear, even phobia about embracing any arrangement involving a meaningful Irish dimension in the current political process. It seems that unionists still fear they will be as much at risk from the Ireland of today as that of 1886.

Some time ago a Presbyterian friend, while visiting a European city with a group from other countries, was asked to participate in a cultural evening. He explained that he was at a loss. As a unionist from Northern Ireland, he was not comfortable with traditional Irish culture. He could not feel included in that. Neither did he see himself as culturally English, Scottish or Welsh and he was not an Orangeman. So he solved his immediate problem by singing a Belfast street song! However, he could identify himself with certainty as a Presbyterian.

This, I think, is the crucial issue for many unionists in relation to their Protestant heritage. When all the other reasons for reaction, opposition and protest against the current political process have been peeled away this, I believe, is the fundamental one, which would remain even if all economic and constitutional objections were resolved.

A Methodist friend of twenty years standing, who is politically nationalist, votes unionist because he perceives the Catholic Church still to be too powerful and dominant an influence in Irish politics. This sentiment within unionism ranges from a wariness and mistrust, to anti-Catholicism in all its forms, where the Catholic Church can be seen to be the greatest threat to Protestantism and unionism, just as they were a threat to each other in the 1860s.

We are credited with, or accused of, having long memories in Northern Ireland! I think this is because we have done one another immense wrongs which we have never sufficiently acknowledged or addressed in the past. The Christian churches, not least my own, and the political parties, not least the Unionist Party, have a great responsibility to give a lead in this respect. Both have wrongs to acknowledge and address.

The responsibility lies with us all to curb our negativity, to promote goodwill and to seek to show it despite those who discourage us. It is our Christian calling to do so. It would be a sign of political leadership at its best and a sign of the mutual esteem we owe one another.

Tom COLLINS

Tom Collins has been editor of the Irish News since 1993. He joined the paper as deputy editor in 1990 following five years on the News Letter. His career began at the Carrickfergus Advertiser in 1983. In 1995 he was named regional newspaper editor of the year, the Irish News was named regional newspaper of the year, and won an outstanding achievement award for its contribution to journalism in the United Kingdom. In 1998 the Irish News and News Letter were jointly awarded the International Federation of Journalists prize for tolerance and understanding in recognition of their initiatives for peace. He is deputy chairman of the Ulster Orchestra.

IN ONE OF THE MOST MEMORABLE EXCHANGES IN MODERN HISTORY, Senator George Mitchell sat across a table from Colonel Oliver North and admonished him with the words, "God does not take sides in American politics."

That is a lesson which has still to be learned on this side of the Atlantic ocean. Our democracy has not matured sufficiently to separate political affiliation from religious belief. There are a few exceptions - Protestant nationalists and Catholic unionists - but their existence tends to prove the rule rather than render it useless.

My very early years were spent in England where my political consciousness could comprehend only the choice between left and right. When my parents moved home to Northern Ireland in 1968 I was sent to the nearby Catholic primary school.

Like most children, we did not get too caught up in the niceties of Northern Ireland politics, but I remember one election provoked debate in the schoolyard about the campaign.

I argued that I would vote for the party which offered the best policies, regardless of religion. I said I would be happy to vote unionist if it would govern best. Surprisingly, I did not get duffed up, but I'm sure my peers regarded me as a bit of an eccentric.

The concept I had transferred from the left-right debate in England was somewhat ahead of its time for Northern Ireland then. It is somewhat chastening to note that the intervening thirty years have made my childhood political thinking no less naive.

Unionism, which remains tied to Protestant institutions such as the Orange Order, has done next to nothing in that period to make itself relevant to Catholics looking for a political home. The same arguments would almost certainly be made by unionists about nationalist parties, though it could be argued that it is easier for a Protestant to be an Irish nationalist than a Catholic to be an Ulster unionist.

From a nationalist standpoint, unionism seems much more fixated on its relationship with Protestantism than nationalism is with Catholicism. For unionists Irish unity is seen not only as a political threat, but a religious one. The notion of a modern Irish government dancing to the tune of the Catholic Church is fanciful. But the 'road to Rome' argument is still a potent one in the unionist's political armoury. I can not think of a single nationalist who sees union with Britain as a threat to his religious freedoms.

At the time of his election as Ulster Unionist Party leader, David Trimble gave some encouraging hints that it was time the party re-evaluated its link with the Orange Order. It may have been well-meant at the time, but if anything the bond between Party and

Order has strengthened rather than weakened. Successive Drumcrees, with the local Church of Ireland as the focal point of opposition, have reinforced the relationship between unionism and Protestantism. And the refusal of Orangemen to sit down with members of host communities to discuss their differences has been underwritten by elected unionist politicians.

It is difficult, too, to disengage party and religion when so many of the key players come complete with dog collars. There are some highly politicised Catholic priests, but none are in electoral politics, and few wield the type of political power enjoyed by the Rev Ian Paisley, the Rev Martin Smyth or the Rev William McCrea.

One could just imagine the suspicion on the unionist side if the leader of the SDLP was a Jesuit priest, the health spokesman of Sinn Fein was a Benedictine monk, or a spokesman of the Workers' Party was a country and western singer.

The concept of *For God and Ulster* undermines both God and Ulster. It would be wrong to take God out of politics. A healthy political life depends on value systems which Christianity provides. But it is essential that we take God out of party politics. It is time unionism found out whether it is capable of standing on its own two feet. *For God* and *For Ulster* are two separate things.

Unionism has disenfranchised the young Catholic schoolboy who wanted only to vote for the party with the best policies. When it addresses that, its claim to speak for 'the greater number' will have some legitimacy.

Oliver CRILLY

Ordained in 1965, Father Oliver Crilly, a native of County Derry, taught in St. Patrick's High School, Maghera. He then spent 13 years in Dublin, first as Director of Veritas Publications, and then as Director of the Catholic Communications Institute of Ireland. In 1982 he returned to the Derry diocese as a curate in the parish of Strabane. Since August 1989 he has been Parish Priest of Melmount, Strabane. He has been a member of the Irish Commission for Justice and Peace and of the Western Education and Library Board. He worked on *Northern Ireland's Prisons: A Report to the Churches* (1990), and on *The Independent Review of Parades and Marches* (The North Report: 1997). He has broadcast frequently in Irish and English, and presented the first Irish language documentary on BBC Television in Northern Ireland. Other interests include leisure cycling, amateur drama and drawing cartoons.

I HAVE FOUND IT EXTREMELY DIFFICULT TO GATHER MY THOUGHTS ON THE subject of Unionism. I don't think it is just because I come from outside the Unionist community. It is also because in my consciousness over the past fifty years or so, Unionism has never been a simple political institution. It has been a complex amalgam of history, politics, religion and social realities, and has been relayed to my Catholic nationalist consciousness through many overlays of symbolism and emotional distortion.

In my pre-teen years, the institutions of the Northern Ireland state and the flavour of Unionist government were mediated to me by the B Specials, who used to stop and question us as we cycled to a Gaelic football match in Gulladuff. Later, when, as a student for the priesthood in Maynooth, I was travelling by the Enterprise Express from Dublin to Belfast on the way home for the Christmas holidays, I was struck by the large 'in-your-face' Union-jack backed official mural proclaiming that "Ulster is British." I wondered who 'they' were trying to convince.

There was a sense of alienation. Unionists were other. When Unionist politicians spoke of 'the people of Ulster,' they clearly didn't mean me or my people. However, realities in Northern Ireland are, and always have been, more complex than the surface images suggest.

My father's first cousin was married to a first cousin of James Chichester Clark. I remember how my political oversimplifications were challenged as I sat in Clarks' in Castledawson and heard my cousins reacting enthusiastically to the appearance of Cousin James - known locally as *the Major* - on television at the Commonwealth Prime Ministers' Conference.

As I wrestled with this question of how I perceived Unionist identity, I came to the conclusion that the most significant thing for me is the degree of change which has taken place during my lifetime, both in Unionism and in my perceptions.

The interesting message for the Unionist leadership is that the more they overstate their case, the less the nationalist community identify with it. Whereas, the more they show concern for equality of treatment and participative structures and attitudes, the more open nationalists will be to cooperation and to a shared vision for the future.

The ten years I spent as a member of the Western Education and Library Board were very formative for me. Before that experience, 'our schools' most likely meant Catholic schools for me. Very soon that had changed, and 'our schools' meant all our schools.

The experience of consensus decision-making and collaborative working for the benefit of all our pupils in the area convinced me that if it can be done in education it can be done in the wider political arena.

There is a religious strand in the question of Unionist identity, and in Catholic perceptions of it. Catholics have not well understood the element of democratic development in the history of British Protestantism, and in the role of King William in particular.

Instead of presenting the positive aspects of that, Unionists have too often leaned on their fears of the political effects of Catholic domination in a united Ireland, and Unionist leaders have too often used slogans like *Home Rule is Rome Rule*, or more vulgar equivalents, to put pressure on their own followers. Fear, like violence, is a very dangerous dynamic for political change or for the prevention of political change.

The great sign of hope for me as I look at Unionism today is that it is no longer a monolith, and that some significant leaders, like David Trimble, seem to have at least begun to realise that the strength of Unionism - in its simplest political meaning of wishing to preserve the British connection - will come from its ability to live with its neighbours in friendship and cooperation, and not from its ability to dominate them.

Austin
CURRIE

A native of Coalisland, County Tyrone, Austin Currie was the youngest MP ever elected to the Stormont Parliament. His squatting in a council house in Caledon is generally recognised as the beginning of the Civil Rights campaign. Along with five other MP's he founded the SDLP in 1970. In 1974 he was Minister for Housing, Planning and Local Government in the Power Sharing Executive. He is currently a Fine Gael TD for Dublin West in Dail Eireann, having served as a Minister of State in the last government. He is unique in being the only person to have served in both Stormont and the Dail and in being a Minister in both jurisdictions.

MY EXPERIENCE OF LIVING AND WORKING IN THE SOUTH HAS confirmed a long held belief that Northeners of the two traditions have more in common with each other than they know, or in some cases are prepared to acknowledge. Tell that to people whose knowledge of Northeners is gleaned mostly from television and they will laugh at you.

Whether Catholics or Protestants, Unionists or Nationalists, we have inhabited the same piece of earth for many generations. We speak with the same accents. Class difference is minimal and where it exists it is built on money or education - tuppence ha'penny looking down on tuppence. We have a common history, though we have different ways of looking at it. We face the same problems; we have the same worries and fears.

Does each community have a distinctive ethos or has such close association blurred historic differences? Take 'the Protestant work ethic', for example - does it exist? From my perspective I think it does. But it has rubbed off on a Catholic community where educational opportunity has created self-confident generations aware of the opportunities and prepared to work hard to achieve them.

Protestants are supposedly more intense - even dour. They drink and gamble less, too concerned with tomorrow's early rising to be gallivanting into the early hours. Certainly the sober suited respectability at Sunday services, and the white gloved, bowler hatted decorousness of the Twelfth, would seem to prove the point. But again, are not the pubs packed on the Twelfth? Are not the queues as long in bookie's shops on Grand National Day in Protestant areas as in Catholic? And is not the Pioneer Total Abstinence Association, with a membership of up to ten per cent of the Catholic population, the largest total abstinence organisation in Northern Ireland?

Many Catholics believe that Protestants are more honest - 'His word is his bond.' Many Protestants believe that too. I have heard it suggested that the practice of confession has had a negative influence on Catholic truthfulness, that the relative ease of forgiveness encourages repetition.

The late Cardinal O'Fiach got himself into hot water by suggesting that Protestant political attitudes were more motivated by religious extremism than were those of Catholics, whose extremism was more political. It is hardly surprising that this should be a Catholic perspective considering how widely held was the belief that *Home Rule is Rome Rule*.

A number of years ago the late Harold McCusker MP gave me an insight into the Protestant psyche when we were in New York together around Saint Patrick's Day. An Orangeman who beat the lambeg drum, he was certainly no dour Protestant and was great company. Not surprisingly he found difficulty in identifying with some aspects of the celebrations in New York.

We agreed there was a wider dimension to his problem. Unionists and Protestants were a majority in Northern Ireland but a minority on the island. And though they considered themselves British, many doubted that a majority of the British reciprocated. Nationalists and Catholics, on the other hand, were a minority in Northern Ireland but a majority on the island. And beyond Ireland they identified with an international diaspora - particularly in the United States - and, of course, a world wide church. Such factors did not contribute to the lessening of a defensive, backs-to-the-wall mentality among Unionists!

As the talks process reached its final stages I veered between hopefulness and optimism that they would be successful. I have long believed that the best way to bring about reconciliation is for representatives of the two traditions to grapple in government with the political, social-economic and cultural problems afflicting the Northern Irish people. That will test my contention that we have much more in common than divides us.

Eoin DE BHALDRAITHE

Eoin de Bhaldraithe (Waldron) was born in County Mayo in 1938, joined the Cistercians in 1956 and was ordained priest (or presbyter) in 1963. He then went to study at the Benedictine College in Rome for two years. There he was taught how to read the Fathers of the Church and received an enthusiastic introduction to ecumenism. Since then he has been at Bolton Abbey where he works on the farm. In his spare time he writes on the eucharist and christology. Ecumenism remains a secondary interest, so he also publishes ideas on intercommunion, mixed marriages, christian peace and the Irish question.

I THINK THAT MOST UNIONISTS WOULD EASILY AGREE THAT THEY ARE SIMPLY protestants. So too nationalists are almost always catholics. As John Whyte reminded us in his 1990 publication, *Interpreting Northern Ireland*, our normal description of the two communities is 'the catholics' and 'the protestants'. The New Ireland Forum Report is one of the few documents that use the 'unionist/nationalist' terminology.

We are talking here about cultural or political catholics and protestants. This is our heritage from the defining moments of the religious wars which ended in the stalemate where everyone in a region was to follow the religion of its ruler. This is why many with little interest in christianity claim to be catholic or protestant.

After the French revolution Irish catholics began to define themselves as republicans. They then claimed non-religious or political motives, and mocked what they saw as the exclusively religious attitudes of protestants. The ultimate farce in this was the

IRA claim that they would not kill a protestant *as* a protestant but *as* something else. Protestants would, however, kill a catholic *as* such.

Whyte also insists that unionists are not British. This designation is claimed by upper class protestants, but only since 1970. Politically, protestants do not want to be ruled by England. The British role is rather to protect them, especially from the catholics. This is cogently argued by D.W. Miller in *Queen's Rebels:Ulster Loyalism in Historical Perspective* (1978). The protestants rely on their paramilitaries when the British seem to be letting them down. Events like the gun running of 1912, the fall of the power sharing Executive in 1974 and, perhaps, Drumcree in 1996 show who holds the power when the crunch comes. The catholics need their paramilitaries on a more constant basis.

Perhaps the protestants are more prone to seek domination over the catholics, whereas the latter say they only want equality. That again is explained historically. The protestants were victorious in the three wars of the seventeenth century, and then were in complete charge for the whole of the next century. History has conditioned them into believing that they should rule by right.

The protestants claim to be democrats but in a suitably defined area. The catholics were in favour of the Union in 1800 as it disbanded the protestant parliament in Dublin. After they got the vote, however, the catholics wanted a parliament again (Home Rule) as they would then be in the majority. The protestants resisted this - whence the designation 'unionist' - until, unexpectedly, in 1920 they got a parliament for an area where they were a secure majority. So by democracy, both mean 'majority rule by us.' For in this kind of contested situation, groups differ in a few well defined areas and tend to assimilate unconsciously to one another in almost everything else.

One difference is the way religion is used. Catholic paramilitaries are often exemplary church goers as this wins political support. A protestant phenomenon is the politician in non-episcopal orders.

The Opsahl Commission found "widespread and deep fear and mistrust" among the protestants about the catholic church. They see catholicism not just as a religion but as "a threatening political system with international dimensions." They believe that "catholicism and Irish nationalism are two parts of the same system." The commission urged the catholic church to do something to allay those fears.

The challenge for us all is, How do we live together? We have tried separation and it has brought us to grief. The coming together could begin if we believing christians were to accept one another as brothers and sisters in the Lord.

Aidan Dolan

Aidan Dolan was born in County Fermanagh and educated at St Michael's College, part-time at The Girls' Collegiate School, Enniskillen, and at Queen's University and the University of Ulster. After working as a stonemason's assistant on York Minster and as a computer programmer in Reading he returned to Northern Ireland. He was Chairperson of the Northern Ireland Council for Integrated Education and has made written and oral submissions to the Opsahl Commission and the Irish Forum for Peace and Reconciliation. He lives in County Tyrone where he is Principal of the Integrated College, Dungannon.

LEARNING UNIONIST IDENTITY - A SECRET DIARY

1956   December

IRA raid Brookeborough Barracks. 'B' men on bikes cycle past our house to intercept attackers twelve miles away. The siren wails at the fire station five hundred yards from my bedroom. (I'm two years old, can I really remember this?)

1960   July 12

Daddy opens our new petrol station as the Twelfth march ends in the field opposite our house. "A good day to start a new business, plenty of people out and about." We sell lots of C & C Orangeade.

1962

Creeping along the hedge that marked the border between our house and our neighbour's, armed with bow and arrows cut from sally rods, we begin our attack. The first salvo fired carries a message, wrapped around an arrow, "We declare war!" It falls unseen in their vegetable patch. Ignored. The Union flag fluttering above their front porch for two weeks in summer is reply enough. "Staunch," someone says. In early morning my sister and I cross the border and eat their peas.

1964

Belleek Customs Officer leans into the car. "Have you anything to declare?" This time the sally arrow's message, timidly launched from the back seat, falls short. Our 'war' is hushed as mammy warns us to be quiet. "The most westerly part of the British Empire," my more learned classmate comments. Beginnings of an intimation that we share the edge of the Union.

1967 March 17

Mr Woods, a neighbour, claims as I fill his petrol tank, "Saint Patrick was a Protestant." Is this a joke?

1970 February 23

Civil Rights protest in Enniskillen. I march and chant. "Tories out North and South, Green and Orange Tories out." Loyalists attack with stones. Definitely, these guys have identity.

1971

'A' level Biology is not taught in St Michael's, so five of us go, part-time, to the Collegiate Grammar School for Protestant girls. The first Catholics, the first boys, to attend. Shy. We hang around their coffee machine at break and try to chat them up. Protestants are easy, its girls that are the hard bit. Ken Adams is the biology teacher, he takes us on a field trip to Portaferry and Strangford Lough - *Fucus vesiculosus* and *Nereis diversicolor* - he seems to want me to learn, no canes, no straps. I learn. Teachers nowadays call it building self-esteem.

1971

Make Love Not War. Lennon and Yoko stay in bed for a week in Amsterdam as a protest gesture against the Vietnam war. I join Enniskillen PACE - Protestant and Catholic Encounter. There are girls there and I seek encounters. Bill Barbour leads the discussion on shared space. Ah, but Enniskillen is not Amsterdam, and there is little enough space sharing of the type most yearned for. John Hewitt and John Montague, The Planter and the Gael, read their poems in Portora Royal School and I listen. An Ulster (Lying) Prophecy, "I saw the Pope breaking stones on Friday...Corks in boats afloat on the summit of the Sperrins...and a curlew in flight surveying a United Ireland." And Hewitt's "no sense flickered through why Europeans, Christians, working class should thresh and struggle in that old morass." No sense makes sense.

Terence Donaghy

Terence Donaghy is a Belfast solicitor and a member of the Northern Consensus Group. Over the last 20 years, he has been increasingly involved with cross-community and inter-church groups. He has been a member of the Community Relations Council and is involved with Columbanus Community of Reconciliation, Restoration Ministries, and with a number of inter-faith prayer initiatives. He is also involved with two recent projects - the *Hand of Friendship* campaign, and *Jesus in the City*.

For a Nationalist to answer the question, What are the distinctive characteristics of the Unionist identity? in a very brief article, is a difficult task. Could I begin by stating my view that my Unionist neighbours are, as a people, a great deal better than the public perception people have of them outside Northern Ireland.

The many reasons why this should be so would themselves be sufficient material for an article. The truth is that the Unionist people now alive in Northern Ireland were born into an immense community problem, in the creation of which they played no part.

Family ties, group loyalty and a shared apprehension of the unknown combined to hinder all but a small minority of them in the task of solving this problem. These were - and are - the internal factors blocking progress.

In addition, there are large and important external factors - the decline of Britain from pre-eminence on the world stage to the role of a relatively minor supporting actor, the development of the European Union, the problems that have beset the Royal Family and caused a large diminution in the almost universal respect they were held in a generation ago, and the greatly improved economic and social position of their Catholic co-citizens (and, incidentally, of the wider Irish Catholic family, both in the Republic and in places like the USA).

As a result of these internal and external factors, Unionists have moved, inside forty years, from being, at least to outward appearances, a secure, stable self-confident majority, to a position of anxiety and concern about the future which, at times, appears to paralyse all efforts aimed at improving their situation. In 1998, the typical Unionist says, or thinks, things like, "Ah, sure, there'll never be any solution here," "The republicans have the Brits in their pockets," "There's no point in talking to the government - they have their minds made up."

But what comes home to me again and again is a feeling that Northern Ireland Unionists are really the same in so many ways as the people in my community. They are, when not threatened in a political way, decent, good-humoured, helpful and humble.

The only difference between your typical Unionist and your typical Nationalist is that the first was born into a community which believed itself destined to rule, and feels that destiny is being steadily eroded to zero, whilst the second was born into a community which saw itself permanently excluded from important social decision making, and now feels that the tide is running in its direction.

Is it any wonder that the first can appear, in public, as dour, serious and ungracious, while the second appears confident, cheerful and creative? But reverse the historic roles, and the above picture would, I have no doubt, be similarly reversed.

Could I end with an insight from a dear friend of mine from the Unionist community? He thinks that hatred of Rome is the biggest factor of all, and describes it as "rank superstition." There might, he feels, have been some small justification for it in days gone by, but there is none now. "Get rid of that, and you'll solve your problem."

Seamus DUNN

Seamus Dunn is Professor of Conflict Studies at the University of Ulster, and Director of the Centre for the Study of Conflict. He was educated in Portstewart, then in St Columb's College, Derry, and studied mathematics at Queen's University, Belfast. He first worked as a teacher of mathematics, and later in teacher education in the University of Ulster in Coleraine. As director of the Centre he has been involved in research on a great many aspects of the social and cultural life of Northern Ireland, including education, religion, mixed marriages, sport, parades, the police, mediation, the voluntary sector and ethnic minorities. He has published very widely on many of these areas and is particularly interested in the role of education in divided societies. He is also a regular broadcaster and journalist.

WHEN I WAS GROWING UP IN PORTSTEWART, THE SEPARATION - such as it was - lay between us, the Catholics, and them, the Protestants. We never heard of unionists or nationalists. They went to the Protestant school and we went to the Catholic school. Our view of them was - impartially - composed of equal measures of ignorance, caution, superiority and fear.

We were profoundly ignorant of what being a Protestant meant, and would have been hard pressed, then or even now, to make a stab at describing the difference between a Presbyterian and a Methodist. We were full of myths and fears about what they did.

There was the Portstewart Convention every year in June, a great white tent that filled up two or three times each day with people in their best clothes carrying bibles. It was a source of great mystery to us, confused with overtones of the circus tent, and made wondrous by the strict injunction never to go near it.

We were not taught to hate Protestants; I have never heard an anti-Protestant sermon in my life, even less in my home. But we were admonished to be cautious; you never knew when some remark might get you into trouble. Even singing the wrong song could be hazardous. However, in school we were taught that we had the good fortune to belong to the 'One, True, Catholic and Apostolic Church'.

The implicit, and indeed sometimes explicit, corollary was that those who did not belong were, at the very least, to be pitied. So we had a sense of the People of God in us, an affirmation of our specialness. This allowed for a sense of superiority - much needed, since much of the other evidence contradicted it. Because these 'inferior' people who were not members of the true church, were, nevertheless, in charge of most of the material things that mattered in our lives. They called the tune in major matters such as getting a house or a job, and in minor ones like getting a signature on an official form, or getting out of the picture house before 'the Queen' was played. These were contradictions in our lives and must surely have contributed to the anger and confusion and thrawn-ness.

Protestants were also clean and tidy people, we were told, and this constituted a sort of challenge to us to do as well. When my mother combed my hair as a boy, she would say, "That's more Protestant looking."

To some extent all of these views changed as I grew older and became aware of, and absorbed by, the long-lived Irish confusion about religion and politics. I learnt that unionist was another word for Protestant and nationalist, for Catholic. And then, later still, that that was nonsense. My first teaching job was in a

Protestant grammar school, where I learnt respect for middle class unionist virtues, and that the word Protestant had many political and religious dimensions and often explained very little.

Thinking about this piece led me to the conclusion that a great deal of what I might write about unionists could just as easily be written about nationalists. This phenomenon is reflected in the continuing demands for any comment about either to be balanced by a similar comment about the other. Writing about unionists, therefore, involves the danger that, without unending qualifications about the other side, I will be accused of believing that anything I might say is unique to unionists. Whereas I have come to believe that, while the nature of commitment may be distinctive or singular, its manifestations are often very similar. There is, however, a greater danger, which is to write as though unionists were a homogeneous body, all alike and all with similar views.

But one sure consequence of the last thirty years has been the knowledge that I do not understand the Northern Ireland virus, along with a determination to allow for the possibility of all sorts of combinations and contradictions. The challenge for all of us, I believe, is to struggle against orthodoxy.

Sean FARREN

Sean Farren was born and educated in Dublin. After qualifying as a teacher he taught in Sierra Leone, Switzerland and Dublin. He undertook postgraduate studies at the University of Essex and accepted a lecturing post at the New University of Ulster in Coleraine in teacher education. A member of the SDLP since the mid-seventies at local and executive level, he has served as party chair. He was a member of the SDLP delegation to the Brooke-Mayhew talks and was a senior negotiator in the multi-party talks following election for the North Antrim constituency in May 1996. He was also elected to the Assembly set up under the Stormont Agreement.

T O THIS OBSERVER FROM A NATIONALIST BACKGROUND THE UNIONIST identity blends a sense of Britishness and Irishness with a religious commitment to Protestantism.

The Britishness of unionists derives both from the historic origins of the people themselves and from their persistent sense of dependence on Britain to sustain and defend them in times of adversity.

Their Irishness is the inevitable product of living in Ireland and of interacting, positively and negatively, with the country's other inhabitants. The accumulated effects of such daily experiences have moulded, and continue to mould, the lifestyles of unionists in ways that are inescapably Irish.

The Protestantism of unionists was an essential characteristic of their forebear's arrival in Ireland and has remained central to their identity. Their Protestantism is seen, historically, to be the source of important civil and religious liberties, as well as a bastion against what are perceived to be the 'evils' of Catholicism. Not the least of these perceptions has been of a Catholic determination to eliminate the Protestant tradition from Irish life.

The extent to which all three elements of the unionist identity are present in any one individual can vary considerably. Some unionists loudly proclaim and celebrate one element more than another. Some almost suppress one. Clearly, for example, some suppress any meaningful religious sense of Protestantism. Others may loudly proclaim one element on one occasion, but over a lifetime give significant expression to all three. Churchgoing unionists who cheer Irish rugby teams with a conviction to rival that of any nationalist supporter exemplify this point.

Like many identities, the relationship between their component elements is not always benign. Depending on circumstances, considerable tension can exist which leads to one or more elements becoming dominant. In recent times, pressure on their Britishness was produced when British governments took action which appeared to large sections of the unionist community to be inimical to their fundamental interests - the Sunningdale and Anglo-Irish Agreements being significant in this respect.

More significantly, for many unionists, IRA violence over the past three decades, together with the general advances made by the nationalist community, seem to have induced a suppression of their Irishness. Fewer unionists today appear prepared to openly acknowledge this element of their identity than was the case in the more tranquil 1960s and earlier.

The essential roots of the unionist identity still lie in the colonial experience of the Protestant settlers in Ulster. From the outset this was an experience of communities of English speaking Protestants living on land confiscated from larger communities of Irish speaking Catholics. The almost inevitable settler-native relationship came to be characterised by suspicion and enmity.

In addition, the policies of the metropolitan power in London led to the settlers' presence being used and abused in the interests of the former. Suspicious of both its benefactor and its immediate Irish-Catholic neighbours, and not powerful enough to fend completely for itself, Ulster Protestantism evolved with what has often been termed a 'siege mentality'.

Notwithstanding uneasy relationships with London, today the political hallmark of the overwhelming majority of unionists is their determination to maintain and strengthen links with Britain within the United Kingdom, and to resist any attempt to force them into unity with the rest of Ireland. Unionists, therefore, proclaim what they believe to be the benefits of UK membership, particularly benefits of an economic, social and cultural kind, while minimising the benefits of all-island links.

To many Nationalists the perceived defensiveness in unionism has inhibited unionists from reaching out to their nationalist neighbours. Violence in pursuit of Irish unity has significantly contributed to this inhibition, as has Nationalists' failure to fully appreciate the true roots and nature of unionist identity.

The lesson to be drawn is that neither community can achieve the security, understanding and respect which it desires without reaching out to the other. Indeed, the security of each community lies essentially in the hands of the other. The Good Friday agreement accommodates the aspirations of both and guarantees their sense of identity. This should be sufficient to assuage the fears of both. Only in such a context will tensions ease to the point where both communities can begin building the future together.

Denis Faul

Right Reverend Monsignor Denis Faul was born in Dundalk in 1932. His father was a County Louth man and his mother a Newry woman. He was educated in St Patrick's College, Armagh and St Patrick's College, Maynooth and ordained as a priest in 1956. He studied in Maynooth for a further year and in Rome for one year. He began his teaching career in St Patrick's Boys' Academy in 1958. He retired in 1998 after forty years at the Academy, fifteen of them as Principal. He is interested in human rights, justice, peace and reconciliation questions. His hobbies are all forms of outdoor games and Modern European languages, although his degree was in Latin and Greek! He likes the 'warm hearted people' of Tyrone and would like to be buried there.

USE YOUR SPADES TO DIG

Unionism is a valid political point of view. The Unionist Party has suffered, having lost the Rev Robert Bradford and Edgar Graham by murderous actions, and living under fear and threat for twenty-seven years. They must be given a feeling of security, a future and a welcome in Ireland, North and South. And they must extend the same to all. Some Catholics are life long Unionists, others are Unionists while they are rearing their children and health and education are free.

The Unionist Party is a diverse party - many MP's hold opinions in public of varying degrees of severity, and in private they hold opinions of varying degrees of kindness and good neighbourliness. In Nationalists' eyes they represent a long history of discrimination in housing, employment and administration of the law. Hopefully that is now changing to fair play and mutual help.

Their leaders have a problem. They are looking over their shoulders at the hard men of 'Ulster', in the same way that Sinn Fein are looking over their shoulders at the hard men of rural and borderland 'Ulster'. If these two groups are both looking over their shoulders at the men of the past is it little wonder that, despite their large votes, they cannot meet and engage with each other about the future?

The hard men call the tune in the Unionist Party and, like the Republicans, one gets more plus marks, the harder one is in opposition. The Loyal Orders wield great influence in the Ulster Unionist Party.

A prominent English politician said about twenty years ago that "the Unionists lack generosity." It was not a very original remark since they base themselves on a 'not an inch' policy in public. Yet privately they speak very differently, they say surprising things like, "There would have been a united Ireland ten years ago, only for the provos," meaning that fear makes them take a hard line. They also talk about agreement, co-operation and local loyalties rather than frontier loyalties. I find this latter attitude encouraging.

If the Unionists would straighten their necks and look forward to the future, and not to the Boyne, they could work out an agreement with their neighbours. An agreement is not a solution. An agreement means that certain lines of procedure can be established and the people can work together on these lines to produce a solution at some future date.

Politicians are elected to represent a political programme, but they have a clear moral duty derived from the basis of democracy and from basic human rights and conscience to represent every person in the constituency. This means helping persons in their day to day problems, as indeed our local MP Ken Magennis does in a diligent fashion for all in Fermanagh and South Tyrone. But it also means an MP does not shut out the political viewpoint of non-Unionists, seeking instead a positive way to engage sympathetically with the good points in it. And he never insults his neighbours or their flag!

Any idea that a majority of one or ten should mean complete domination of Committees, Boards and the like, without allowing participation from a 'minority'(!) of forty-five percent, belongs to the mind set of not so innocent tyrants. An MP or councillor is primarily a public representative and must represent all the people.

'All politics are local politics' is a true saying which the Unionist Party in Dungannon has recognised through voluntary power sharing. Hopefully, Unionists will extend this policy to produce a sense of equality and fair play in the whole community.

There is no grand Moses type solution, brought down from on high on two stone tablets by Mr Trimble and Mr Hume, to the problems of Northern Ireland. Each small town or area must work out its own peaceful and prosperous existence and use the talents of all its people in harmonious co-operation and respect to survive, when the European money has gone elsewhere.

When all the rich 'uncles' have left the scene, Nationalists and Unionists must take spades and dig their native soil for a living and not attack each other with the spades!

Padraic Fiacc

Padraic Fiacc is the pen name of Patrick Joseph O'Connor. He was born in Belfast in 1924, but moved to New York with his family in 1929. He returned to Belfast, where he still lives, in 1946. His publications include *Missa Terribilis* (1988), *Ruined Pages* (1994), *Red Earth* (1996) and *Woe to the Boy* (1997). His honours include the George Russell (AE) Memorial Prize and the Poetry Ireland Prize. He is a member of Aosdana.

IN THE EARLY CHRISTIAN CHURCH SEGREGATION, TO THE PITCH OF ALMOST disintegration, loomed under even the unifying guidance of the sagacious Saint Paul, who appealed:

I do appeal to you brothers for the sake of our Lord, Jesus Christ, to make up the differences among yourselves to be united again in your belief and practice. It is clear that there are serious differences among you. What I mean are all these slogans that you have. "I am for Paul." "I am for Appollos." "I am for Cephas." "I am for Christ." Has Christ been parcelled out? Was it Paul that was crucified for you? Were you baptised in the name of Paul?

Although I lived most of my 73 years here in Belfast where I was born, I had a Roman Catholic education in New York for which I remain, to this day, very grateful. Yes, I deviated betimes - taking Holy Communion in a Russian church downtown (near Little Italy), or attending services with my Protestant friends in their own churches which we were not allowed to do at that time.

In my Catholic education and training, history played a key part. We were taught that Catholicism was for unity and Protestantism was for the individual. As a poet I tended to side with the individual and believed indeed, and still do, that nothing tends more to express the universal than the individual - as for instance the concrete detail feeds poetry as a symbol rather than the philosophical abstract word.

An English poet, Thompson, author of *The Hound of Heaven*, wrote that what the saint is to the theologian the poet is to the philosopher - in short, the poet and the saint act whilst the theologian and philosopher merely speculate. Which finally brings me round the road to concrete historical unionism in the context of our comparatively new state of present day Northern Ireland.

If I'm tempted into the realms of philosophy at all, I would tend as a poet towards the phenomenal forms of existentialism - a kind of umbrella belief underneath which everything that befalls us, everything that we are (subjectively) has an objective existence, apart from ourselves, on a symbolic plane.

To me, humanity has always tended towards unity. First there is man and woman, then the family, the tribe, then the union of the tribes - the nation. Even nationalists are 'unionists' seeking a united Ireland, while unionists seek a united Britain and Ireland.

In our day we have the United Nations, the United States and a coming together even in our present day Europe. The world grows smaller and there is a greater sense of human community - especially during the latter part of our own century with the communications revolution.

What has to be curbed is a forced unity brought about by brute force or violence, if we humans learn from our own history at all - and alas, sometimes at what a cruel savage price? Even in our very own century - the evils of political enslavement of millions and millions of our fellow human beings, the mental and physical torture and downright slaughter, Nazi Germany, Soviet Russia, and the list could be extended ...

This is where the Christian concept should warn and, indeed, warm us like the sun. The ancient Arabs say, "There is no God but God."

"Give us the hope of love O God, the hope you gave us when you gave us your son, Jesus Christ." And to hearken to Saint Paul again, "The greatest of all this hope is love."

Now to get off my soapbox and sink to my youthful New Yorkese - disunity is everwhere: here in our wounded town, Belfast, die-hard splinter groups are splitting up and carrying on their own individual wars.

Peace! How do you get peace? Peace is a state of mind. Christ said it all, "Love God and love each other as you love yourselves."

Brian
LAMBKIN

Brian Lambkin joined Lagan College, Belfast - Northern Ireland's first planned integrated school - at its foundation in 1981. He was Princpal from 1993 until 1997. Now he is Director of the Centre for Migration Studies at the Ulster American Folk Park, Omagh. His book, *Opposite Religions Still? Interpreting Northern Ireland after the Conflict*, was published in 1996.

D EEP DOWN IN THE FOUNDATIONS OF UNIONIST IDENTITY LIES THE belief that Catholics belong to an 'opposite religion'. How variously this deep belief is manifested today by individual unionists is evident from contributions to the volume which precedes this one, *Faith in Ulster*.

As the introduction wisely observes, there is no unionist monolith but a spectrum. That spectrum is differentiated most clearly by how unionists respond to the key question, Do Catholics belong to the same religion as us, or do they belong to an 'opposite religion'? Three main types of response can be distinguished in the contributions to *Faith in Ulster*.

The first type is certain that Protestantism is the 'true religion' and that Roman Catholicism is a 'false' or 'opposite religion'. For example, Gareth Burke says, "I am fully committed to the Protestant reformed religion...I am opposed to the doctrine and worship of the Church of Rome and abhor all forms of ecumenism." David McConaghie says, "I am against Roman Catholicism which I consider an idolatrous and blasphemous religion."

Not all committed Protestants and unionists are comfortable with such certainty. The second type of unionist response remains more or less committed to the exclusive claims of Protestantism, but shows signs of shifting towards an approach more inclusive of Roman Catholicism. It is more inclined to see idolatry and blasphemy in the extreme Protestant position.

As Chris Wright expresses it, "I share my fellow Ulster Protestants' heritage and faith...but I am ashamed of some aspects of that politico-religious culture...some are so suffused with demonic hatred that to say it is for God I consider blasphemous."Roy Garland, Finlay Holmes, Mark Houston, Roy Magee and Ian Major all distance themselves from elements in the Protestant and unionist heritage which they identify as idolatrous or blasphemous.

The third type of unionist response has shifted to a position that is inclusive of Roman Catholicism. From a more or less religious perspective, Protestantism and Catholicism are seen not as opposite religions but as parts of the same religion. Fred Catherwood speaks of "the Christian faith." Ken Bloomfield refers to "basic tenets of the religion most of us share," and Robin Eames to "a God for all the people of this divided community...who transcends the barriers."

From a more or less secular perspective Will Glendinning says that he wants the phrase *For God and Ulster* "to encompass all the traditions - to be inclusive." Michael Hall says, "My heritage is global, one that connects me to cultures far beyond these shores;" and Philip Orr says, "For God and Ulster may be where I started from, but it is not where I have ended up."

The process of shift across the spectrum of the three types of response is described by David Hewitt. Formerly he was an 'opposite religions' man, "easily persuaded that the real enemy of the Kingdom of God was the Roman Catholic Church." Then he discovered "practising Catholics whose commitment to Jesus Christ and the Scriptures was undeniable." The shift was gradual: "I took opportunities to have fellowship with such people, reluctantly at first. I can only say that these experiences, though culturally uncomfortable to begin with, were immensely liberating."

Hewitt, like Catherwood, Bloomfield, Eames, Glendinning, Hall and Orr, have, as it were, 'emigrated' from an earlier position where Catholicism is still seen as an 'opposite religion'. It is significant that the shift in Hewitt's position came about through personal contact with Catholics. We can see why those like Burke and McConaghie disapprove of mixed marriage and integrated education.

Pace Michael Longley, who says, "The fact that our children are still not educated together has little to do with God;" in fact it has a lot to do with God. It has to do with the belief deep down in the foundations of unionist identity that Catholics belong to an 'opposite religion'.

Brian
LENNON

Brian Lennon is a Jesuit priest currently living in Armagh. He spent the last year studying in the US and he also spent some time in South Africa attending sessions of the Truth and Reconciliation Commission. He is a founder member of the Interchurch Group on Faith and Politics and author of *After the Ceasefires: Catholics and the Future of Northern Ireland* (1995).

I VERY MUCH WELCOME THE INVITATION FROM **ECONI** TO CONTRIBUTE to this book. It is a sign of the times that an evangelical group can ask a Jesuit priest for his views on Unionism. All over Northern Ireland people from different backgrounds are coming together to share and exchange their different values and experiences. I am convinced that those experiences are the cement that will build and ultimately hold together any future peace.

I would like to hang my comments around the themes of visibility and invisibility. I believe our future lies only in allowing ourselves to see and accept the different groups - with all their differences - which inhabit this island. Our temptation is to pretend, or to wish, that these groups did not exist.

One of the positive changes in Unionism in recent years has been the emergence of the new political parties. These have shown a new face of Unionism which is all the more remarkable given the appalling paramilitary background from which they come.

As I understand them, they take Nationalists seriously, even though they obviously disagree with them on key issues. They are committed to an agenda of equality, and they are grimly aware of how working-class Unionists have been hoodwinked by the self-serving middle-class ideology which dominated sections of Unionism in the past. They are determined to make visible the economically marginalised within the Protestant and Unionist community, who have been made invisible by the conflict between green Nationalism and the negative side of British Unionism. They are by far the most interesting and hopeful political group on the island, however small they may be as yet.

Overall, however, what most Nationalists see in Unionism are efforts at domination, and they see the differential in employment rates, Unionist domination of the Police, Orange marches, and Unionist symbols of the State as symptoms of this domination.

Of course this is a highly selective and one-sided picture, and to that extent it reflects the basic sin of many of us in Northern Ireland - a refusal to step into the shoes of the other tradition and to understand their fears.

Many Nationalists still have no idea of the deep insecurity felt by many Unionists: the almost fatalistic belief that we are heading to a United Ireland (a belief which in my view flies in the face of political realities), the fear that Northern Ireland will end up dominated by the Catholic church, a sense that Unionist British identity will be swept away, that those in the Police who held the line against the IRA will receive no recognition for their sacrifices, and in the end will simple lose their jobs like so many other Unionists simply to appease Nationalists.

I think Nationalists have to hear and understand these fears, however much they disagree with them. But Unionists also need to hear Nationalist fears. At the moment a central aspect of Unionist identity seems to be fear of the future, while a central aspect of Nationalist identity is resentment at all that Northern Ireland stands for. Both sides have to change it we are going to make a future.

Finally, a necessarily brief comment on the role of religion. In both traditions religion has played a major role in binding the community together. But as with the Israelites of old and with every human society since, religion can be used as a means of opposing the God revealed by Jesus of Nazareth. It is often used as a way of providing false security, security against the fear of death, or of isolation, or of other loss. Faith in Jesus Christ does not necessarily provide security against any of these. It puts its ultimate trust in Christ, no matter what happens.

For me the difference between religion and faith is the difference between blockers and searchers. Blockers want to block out questions, especially those raised by people who differ from *us*. Searchers never end seeking the mystery which lies in us, because, ultimately, that is one of the best ways we can glimpse the mystery that is God.

As I see it, the sin in the religious element of Unionism is to be too closely tied to a political ideology. Connected with this are two other temptations. The first temptation is towards respectability. Tax collectors may find a place in Protestant churches, but where are the prostitutes or their equivalent?

The second is a glorification of militarism: we not only honour those who have died in wars, we often do so in a way which makes it more likely that others will follow in their footsteps. Is it really appropriate to have military banners in churches?

I am of course deeply aware of our own faith failings within the Nationalist community and my own Roman Catholic church. Perhaps our biggest failing has been to see ourselves only as victims and to overlook the Gospel call to take responsibility for our political future - together with our Unionist brothers and sisters.

Unionism has many positive elements in it. Its founding event was the victory of the Boyne, which in its historical context was a victory for parliament, and therefore democracy, over against domination by the monarch. Human rights should therefore be an easy theme for Unionists to relate to.

Secondly, honesty, uprightness and truth are central elements in Northern Ireland Protestantism. We Catholics tend to play easy with words. Indeed we take delight in ambiguity.

Thirdly, in recent decades in the Catholic church we have - quite properly I think - emphasised the human Christ. But we must not lose sight of the Lordship and transcendent nature of God. If perhaps we have something to offer Protestants about Christ's human nature, then they have much to teach us about God's mystery and glory.

As in so many other areas, if we only listened to each other we could learn from each other and offer each other help. I look forward to learning more about the Unionist and Protestant community in the future, and again I thank ECONI for their initiative in bringing out this book.

Pat McArt

Pat McArt is Group Editor of Derry Journal Group Newspapers Ltd. He is a former journalist in the political unit in RTE in Dublin. He was born and reared in Donegal. He describes himself as a 'liberal Catholic'.

I HAVE KNOWN MANY PROTESTANT PEOPLE IN MY LIFE. BY AND LARGE I found them honest, decent and honourable. But I don't claim to understand all of their beliefs. Indeed, at the more extreme end I have a constant running battle with a 'born again' journalistic colleague who firmly believes that 'if you are saved in the Lord Jesus Christ' the rest doesn't matter - you are on the way to the promised land.

"But what about saving starving children?" I frequently ask. "Does a 'born again' walking past a starving child who makes no effort to help get to heaven?"

"Ah," he always replies, "there go you Catholics again. You confuse good works with being saved."

It's a circular argument that I never seem to win. And then it gets even more confusing when politics and religion are inter-twined.

Take, for example, the giant shadow cast in both the religious and political life of Northern Ireland by Dr Ian Paisley. This is the man who used to proclaim - and probably still does - that *Home Rule* in Ireland would mean *Rome Rule*, and that Protestants would find themselves subjected to laws enacted at the whim of 'the harlot of Rome' if ever they had the misfortune of having a united Ireland foisted upon them.

Leaving aside the broader political question, I never cease to be amazed at the capacity for double-think of not only Dr Paisley, but also his not inconsiderable number of supporters. Here is a clergyman, the leader and founder of the Free Presbyterian church, an MP at Westminster, and an MEP and there he is - along with colleagues such as the Rev William McCrea and the Rev Ivan Foster and not forgetting the Ulster Unionist Party's Rev Martin Smyth - warning Protestants to be alert to the dangers, and the pernicious influence, of churchmen interfering in the politics of the state.

I suppose Dr Paisley's views, in many ways, outline in sharp relief the way nationalists view unionism and religion. When Dr Paisley tops the poll in the European elections, on each occasion the lines between unionist politics and the Protestant religion become blurred for many nationalists. Is he getting that huge vote for his political views? For his religious view? Or for a combination of both?

By way of marked contrast, more and more one sees a very clear delineation between nationalism and the Catholic church. The old certainties in the Catholic/nationalist tradition are gone.

In the Republic, births outside of marriage are now commonplace, divorce is permissible, contraception is so widespread even its ritual condemnation has fallen into disuse, and the influence of the church has waned to such a degree that even some of the more liberal commentators are beginning to publicly theorise that perhaps it has all gone to far. Those are, by any gauge, radical changes.

But where is the counterbalancing radicalism within unionism? In his contribution to *Further Afield: Journeys from a Protestant Past* (1996) the academic and film-maker, Desmond Bell, made the point, "Within the Protestant community in Northern

Ireland there is at present no room for dissenting voices, and for those who would question the prevailing unionist hegemony."

In fact, it seems to most nationalists that it is those who demand absolute adherence to the old ways who gain most kudos from the unionist electorate and the Protestant people. Despite none of his party's MP's voting for him, David Trimble's performance at Drumcree ensured his election as UUP leader. And Dr Paisley hardly qualifies as the Ken Livingstone of Ballymena. These leaders appeal to the heartland on an agenda that is premised on both religious and political fundamentalism.

There seems little room for liberalism in either unionism or Protestanism. Liberalism, it would seem, is perceived as both dangerous and weak, whereas being reactionary and right wing is regarded as safe and strong.

It would seem that the siege mentality in unionism and Protestanism remains a potent weapon. It is hard to build bridges with people who perceive you as the enemy. My hope is that people like David Ervine and Billy Hutchinson are reflective of a new breed of unionist/loyalist, people who are not scared of nationalists or Catholics.

Churches should be used for praying in, politics should be kept for political forums. The less the two are inter-twined the more chance there is of political progress.

Patrick McCafferty

Father Patrick McCafferty is a priest of the Diocese of Down and Connor. Since his ordination in 1989, he has ministered in the Parishes of St Patrick, Downpatrick, the Nativity, Poleglass and, currently, Holy Trinity, Turf Lodge.

MY EARLIEST PERCEPTIONS OF UNIONISM WERE NOT VERY positive. My first eight years, from 1963 to 1971, were spent in Rathcoole estate in north Belfast. At that time the estate had an almost equal number of Catholics and Protestants. Then violence and unrest erupted and we, along with so many other Catholic and Protestant families, suffered the trauma of being driven from our home under threat of sectarian attack and made refugees.

However, I did not, at that time, see the Protestant faith as being in any way tied to the aggressive expression of Unionism that often paraded past our house in combat style uniform, waving flags and wielding various forms of weaponry.

Rathcoole Methodist Church was at the top of our street. I remember going in there on a number of occasions as a child and not being particularly conscious that it was all that different from our own Parish Church, except that it was a more modern building. It too was a holy place where I was conscious of God's presence.

My parents and teachers, while giving me a deep love for my Catholic faith, never highlighted the differences that existed between Catholic and Protestant. After we had to leave Rathcoole, we moved to Whiteabbey, my mother's home place. Whiteabbey village was a fairly well integrated community. I was privileged to have many Protestant friends and neighbours when I was growing up and, generally speaking, we got on well. That is not to say that the tragic events unfolding in Northern Ireland did not arouse deep emotions, tensions and, at times, hostility.

I was becoming more familiar with the reasons for the animosity that was wreaking such havoc and devastation across the community. I was also introduced to its religious dimension. Someone posted a tract through our letterbox attacking various tenets of the Catholic faith. It was my first exposure to the vituperative and nasty anti-Catholic literature that is common in these parts.

During my life thus far and through various circumstances and encounters that have come my way in recent years as a priest, I have often met the unpleasant face of the Protestant/Unionist identity in Northern Ireland. It can be a strange and ambiguous mix of religion and politics - a heady brew. There is, in some quarters, a lack of humility, deep-seated hatred, dismissive arrogance, suspicion, inhumanity and intolerance. There is a stubborn refusal to engage properly with others and a failure to listen respectfully to their stories.

As a Catholic community we frequently experience a contempt that is so insidious it is practically subconscious. There is a very strident and vociferous manifestation of the Unionist identity that is elitist and separatist, viewing all aspects of our community with scorn and abhorrence. For many years, as Catholics, we have found ourselves living in a society where we were unwelcome and unvalued.

Nevertheless, I have also been graced over the years with the friendship of many Protestant and Unionist people who have taught me the value of their own spiritual and political traditions. I think we are beginning to see the emergence of a more Nationalistfriendly Unionism that is being gradually freed from its jingoist, factional and imperialistic baggage.

Our problems in this society stem from the disorder of broken relationships: between Westminster and Dublin, between the peoples of Ireland, North and South, between Catholic and Protestant, Unionist and Nationalist. All of us have a role in unravelling the confusion and healing the wounds. Whether we like it or not, we are in relationship with one another. We are neighbours and, as such, we are commanded by Christ to love one another. We are all created in God's image and likeness.

Among the most lethal of all falsehoods that can afflict Christians are the sanctification of prejudice and the canonisation of bigotry. It is simply not an option, for those of us who claim to be followers of Jesus Christ, to view each other with either open hostility or a begrudgery that barely tolerates the other's existence. The call to be reconciled, to really open our hearts to God's Spirit, is compulsory for Christians.

The healing Spirit of the Lord, if we dare to allow him, can expand our constricted hearts and prize open our eyes to see beyond that narrowness of vision which quickly becomes darkness.

Cal McCrystal

Cal McCrystal was born in Belfast in 1935 and educated in Roman Catholic schools. After a spell with the Belfast Telegraph, he worked for The Sunday Times in London and New York before becoming, in turn, that newspaper's news editor, foreign editor and senior features writer. He joined the Independent on Sunday in 1990, leaving five years later to write for The Observer. He has broadcast in Britain, Ireland, the United States and Canada and written for publications in those countries and in Australia. Co-author of *Watergate, The Full Inside Story* (1973), his highly-acclaimed *Reflections On A Quiet Rebel (1997)*, a memoir about Northern Ireland before the Troubles, won the 1998 Belfast Arts literary award. A member of the editorial board of the British Journalism Review, he lives in London.

IN MARCH 1998 WE WERE ASKED TO SALUTE EUROPEAN BRAIN DAY. I doffed my hat. A good reason to celebrate the cerebrum, I concluded, was its display some weeks earlier of extraordinary resilience to violent attack, a young woman passenger on a London suburban train having survived the full penetration of her brain by a mugger's knife. A surgeon described this as a miracle. Others might call it perversity.

I thought of Descartes, who guessed that the soul was located in the pineal gland. This, in turn, prompted a brief reverie in which I contemplated various attempts to drill the brain down the centuries: political brainwashing, unfashionable today; 'dumbing down', currently prevailing; and religion, always with us. All three, in my view, are impediments to truthful exploration. And in Northern

Ireland, the first and the third have been - and continue to be - powerful co-conspirators.

As a young Catholic man in Belfast, I read that the Jewish Rationalist Berner once described dogma as a source of disunion, but added that the ancient ritual observances preserve a common *esprit de corps*. I agreed with this, though took no comfort from it, because *esprit de corps* in religious practice and thought (to the extent that I was able to monitor them) seemed little different from exhortations to make separate and to exclude - on both sides of the 'divide'. Steadfastness, generally admired as a virtue, can equal obstinacy, generally deplored as a fault. What offended me, as I observed 'stalwart' Unionists and 'devout' Nationalists, was *pertinaciam et inflexibilern obstinationem*, traits which Pliny detected in the Scillitan Martyrs.

In retrospect, I find that those Ulster Protestants with whom I felt most comfortable (and, I would surmise, felt similarly with me) were either unpassionate in their religious faith or, if passionate, privately so. They never would dream of brandishing their Christianity as a weapon capable of excising another Christian's frontal lobe or saving whatever might repose within his pineal gland.

But the brand of Protestantism that has sustained many Unionists *was* brandished. It inspired both the Bible-thumper and the ordinary thumper, not to console 'the minority' but to intimidate it. Consequently, Unionism gained, beyond Ulster and in England particularly, a reputation for churlishness, lack of sensitivity and imagination that was not always entirely justified, but has pursued it since.

Dogmatism tended to deny dialogue, while Truth (which I once had considered to be religion's vestment) was pulled aside in favour of a display of Power. In the opening essay of *Power and the*

Church - Ecclesiology In An Age of Transition (1998) Martyn Percy says, "Power is the ability of its holders to carry out their will, exact compliance, exert force and compel obedience...In any consideration of politics or society, the subject of power (and its legitimacy) is never far from the surface."

Percy was addressing neither Northern Ireland's problems nor its churches. But his words can be applied with strong effect to my native province where Protestant churches have, in one way or another, hitched themselves to the power of a Protestant state. There is nothing so ungodly than to witness a Protestant clergyman telling a congregation or public meeting that all who do not cling to his views are condemned to everlasting torment, beginning immediately if at all possible.

I know there are innumerable Protestant clerics who condemn such rants. Yet they are to be criticised for allowing, by default down the years, the hue of Ulster Unionism to be one of intolerance and bigotry, as often as not wearing a sash and walloping a drum. Unionism has always tended to blur its perfectly reasonable case by enveloping it in religious and sectarian vapouring, noxious to some and irrational to others. Nothing, I sometimes feel, has changed in Northern Ireland since Herbert of Cherbury, in the days of Charles I, denounced bitterly the provinciality of Christian controversies.

Too often the heart of Unionism's churchgoer has been deliberately and malevolently stoked to furnace-heat by Protestant fundamentalists, making social pluralism all but impossible. I doubt that I shall be doffing my hat again this year. For, as someone (Clement of Alexandria possibly?) once concluded

> *Ah yet, when all is thought and said,*
> *The heart still overrules the head.*

Noel
McKeown

Noel Mc Keown, OP was born in Derry and grew up in Belfast. He joined the Dominican order in 1959 in Cork and has served in Australia and Ireland. He is currently attached to his Order's house in Newbridge in County Kildare. A firm believer in Christian unity, he is convinced that people in Northern Ireland are more united than they imagine and should declare that unity to the world and reject the title of a divided society.

U NIONIST MEANS SOMEONE WHO WISHES TO REMAIN PART OF THE United Kingdom of Great Britain and Northern Ireland. That is a matter of choice and one which people are free to make.

Those who do make this choice are usually protestant, though, in my view, the choice has nothing to do with religion . The question therefore is, What is a protestant? My understanding of the term is someone who believes in Jesus Christ and in his word.

Protestants are therefore Christians and members of the church of Christ. In this sense they are united with millions of Christians world-wide and hope to bring the message and power of Christ to everyone everywhere.

The protestant tradition uses the bible as its starting point and moves from there to find its role in life and in the world.

As part of the Christian church, it is aware of the wish of Christ that all his followers be one just as Jesus and the Father are one. It therefore earnestly seeks the will of Christ that all followers of his be one and act as he wishes them to act in their lives day by day.

Protestants read the bible. They regard it as God's word for them and indeed for everyone. They look to it for guidance and inspiration. They use it as a prayer book, reciting the psalms and other prayers found in its pages. They wish everyone to read and meditate on the message of its books.

Protestants are people of prayer. They pray to God and to Jesus Christ his Son and to the Holy Spirit who is the love of the Father and the Son for each other. They pray privately or together in church and other places. They pray for themselves and for others, as Christ taught in the bible.

Protestants are people of action. They work as God commanded, serving their neighbour in all walks of life, seeing their work as a service done for Christ and through Christ. Protestants are workers. In all this they are finding their place as members of the church of Jesus Christ. God the Holy Spirit, who dwells in their hearts and who constantly moves them to work for him and for others, is enlightening them.

Protestants are talkers! That is to say that they talk to their neighbours and to everyone and are especially keen to talk to Christians who are fellow members of Christ's church. They are eager to promote understanding of the faith and of the church of which they are baptised belongers.

Protestants are singers in that they sing the praise of God and worship him in services punctuated by psalms and hymns of praise. They espouse the gifts of the Holy Spirit and use them for themselves and for others who wish to benefit from their use.

Protestants are students of the word of God. They follow the example of their Jewish counterparts who study the bible and seek with them and with other Christians the will of God and the understanding of his message for themselves and for others in every part of the world.

Protestants are people of peace. Christ willed that everyone should love his neighbour, so protestants try to live up to that and bear witness to the example of Christ himself. They are willing to lay down their lives for Christ and for anyone who needs assistance.

Protestants are people of enterprise because the world needs many things like health and education, so they are to be found at all sorts of research and business initiatives - this at the service of humankind.

May their work, their love, their hope bring education, health and good life to many now and forever in heaven.

Paddy MONAGHAN

Paddy Monaghan is Secretary of Evangelical Catholic Initiative in the Republic of Ireland, involved in promoting renewal in the Catholic Church, fostering reconciliation among Christians and building Jewish-Christian relationships. He is a Reconciliation Facilitator funded under the Programme for Peace and Reconciliation. He is the co-editor, with Eugene Boyle, of *Adventures in Reconciliation: Twenty-Nine Catholic Testimonies* (1998).

A SOUTHERN EVANGELICAL CATHOLIC'S PERSONAL PERCEPTION OF THE ULSTER PROTESTANT

OF THE **1.6** MILLION PEOPLE IN NORTHERN IRELAND, SOME **900,000** would identify themselves as Protestants. I understand from various sources that some 250,000 of these would identify themselves as 'evangelical'. About 40% of these (comprising Free Presbyterians, most Baptists, Brethren and significant numbers of Presbyterians) would tend to view the Roman Catholic church as a non-Christian church, on a par with, for example, the Mormons. They would look upon the Pope as a manifestation of anti-Christ, and maintain that if a Catholic becomes a born-again Christian he must leave the Catholic Church. Of the remaining 60%, an increasing number would not want to be identified as 'evangelical' as they strongly object to the perceived narrow fundamentalism and bigotry of the 40%. Many are taking significant steps to find their brothers and sisters in Christ within the Roman Catholic church.

Since 1973 when I came in a personal way to accept Jesus as my Lord and Saviour, I have come to appreciate some of the wonderful strengths in the Protestant community, while being aware of shortcomings and injustices that helped give rise to the Troubles. There are also great strengths and weaknesses in the Catholic community. I am convinced that if both communities can rediscover the Lord Jesus Christ, and in Him find each other, then a genuine spiritual revival will sweep Ireland. I believe that God's word to Israel carries hope for our situation in Ireland:

"If my people who are called by my name will humble themselves ...then I will ...heal their land" (2 Chronicles 7.14)

Some things I admire about Protestants are:

Verbal Directness Protestants tend to say exactly what they think.

Loyalty Protestants tend to put a high value on loyalty in relationships: in business, to their community, to the Crown.

Evangelical Faith This is a great strength - the commitment of Protestants to bringing people into a living relationship with our Lord Jesus, their love for Scripture and their desire to be faithful to obeying God's word.

Radical Thinking Some Presbyterians were instrumental in setting up the United Irishmen in the eighteenth century. Recently some key initiatives have come from former loyalist paramilitaries, through the PUP and UDP. The formation and witness of ECONI has been such an encouragement in applying gospel values, as has the courage of ministers like Sam Burch, Ken Newell and others who engaged with Sinn Fein and sought to be witnesses for the Gospel.

Fairness There is a basic sense of fairness. Dr Paisley has the deserved reputation in his constituency of fighting as hard for Catholic constituents as for Protestant ones.

Some less admirable traits are:

Reactionary Fear of the Roman Catholic Church This is encapsulated in the cry *Home Rule is Rome Rule*. It has not been entirely groundless, given, for example, the *Ne Temere* Decree (1907), demanding a written undertaking that children of mixed marriages be raised as Catholics, or the declaration by Cardinal McRory in 1931 that "the Protestant Church in Ireland was not even a part of the Church of Christ," a sentiment reciprocated by many Protestants. It is worth noting the apology recently given by Bishop Willie Walsh for the damage done by the *Ne Temere* Decree.

The assertion in the Westminster Confession of Faith that the Pope is the anti-Christ has greatly influenced Protestantism. While many Presbyterians have distanced themselves from this statement, many others in the Protestant community have thus been blinded to the reformation happening this century in the Catholic Church. This is evidenced by Vatican II and by many Protestant - Catholic dialogues, such as the Reformed Churches - RC Dialogue (1984-1990), which resulted in agreement on justification by faith. There are also ongoing initiatives at grass roots like the recent *Evangelicals and Catholics Together in Ireland* statement endorsed by 130 clergy and lay leaders, including 40 evangelical Catholics.

Inflexibility Protestants tend to want things cut and dried and are suspicious of a Catholic culture that gives such a high priority to maintaining relationships. It seems the Anglo-Irish Agreement, Downing Street Declaration and, latterly, the Good Friday Agreement were written in a language some Protestants find hard to understand. These documents were devised to allow for latitude, something which Protestants find difficulty in coping with.

Historical Tendency to Create and Maintain Divisions There is a well-documented tendency in Protestantism to divide over any perceived betrayal of principle, rather than accommodate conflicting diversity. Theological issues take priority over the issue of unity.

An Inability to Empathise with Fellow Citizens from the Catholic Tradition There is a widespread inability to appreciate Irish culture and history. Many Protestants seem not to understand that, for their Catholic neighbours, what resulted from the Battle of the Boyne has been a history of dispossession and humiliation. The reality is that you cannot love your neighbour and celebrate his defeat at the same time. There has also been a failure to comprehend how threatened Catholics felt by the Unionist majority, backed up by the might of Britain, and how they felt themselves to be second-class citizens.

Confused Identity The Protestant community seems largely to be a people in search of identity. They are definitely not English, Scots or Welsh, yet not fully Irish.

Reluctance to Admit Social Injustice There has been a lack of concern in the Protestant community for social justice. They seemed largely unaware of the increasing anger within Nationalists concerning discrimination. It was a considerable shock when they found themselves, through the Civil Rights campaign in 1968, vilified in the world press for bigotry and discrimination. Not only were electoral boundaries gerrymandered, but housing was manipulated to consolidate Unionist power. The Protestant churches did not necessarily agree with such practices, but said little about them.

Prejudice Many evangelical Protestants express such patronising prejudices as 'Catholics can't be Christians,' 'the Catholic Church is not a Christian church,' 'Catholics believe in salvation by works,' 'for Catholics, grace is mediated by Mary,' 'Catholics believe there is no salvation outside their Church,' 'the Mass is blasphemy and no born again Christian can partake in it.'

For too long Protestants have tolerated such attitudes. Surely we need to get back to the viewpoint of the Reformers, who held that the Catholic church was a Christian church, though standing in need of renewal and reformation. Surely every Christian tradition in Ireland also stands in need of ongoing renewal and reformation.

Many evangelical Protestants hold views of the Catholic church which I believe are unfair, unscriptural and often contemptuous, such as the belief that the Pope is the anti-Christ. Such views preclude reconciliation from their agenda. Unlike the Reformers, whom they profess to admire and follow, they do not engage in dialogue with Catholic Christians at local level.

Some weaknesses are common to both communities. Both are marked by a sexism that plays down the role and importance of half of the Body of Christ. I think it was essential for the Good Friday Agreement that Northern Ireland had a female Secretary of State in Dr Mowlam. Both traditions have also mixed politics and religion.

In conclusion, I believe that in the mutual sharing of our testimonies there is a key to learning to appreciate each other and changing the negative aspects of our identities. This is an effective way for born-again Christians within the Catholic and Protestant churches to find each other (see Revelation 12.14). For this reason I co-edited a recent book - *Adventures in Reconciliation* - giving my testimony and that of 28 other evangelical Catholics, all of whom are involved in building bridges of friendship with Protestant Christians.

The challenge for all born-again Christians in both communities is to build friendships together. If we will do this, Ireland can again become a light to the nations.

Frank
MULLAN

Father Frank Mullan CM was born in Coleraine, County Derry.
Educated in St Columb's College, Derry and St Patrick's College,
Maynooth, he joined the Vincentian Community in 1945 and was
ordained priest in 1950. He taught in St Paul's College, Raheny,
Dublin. Later, he worked as a missionary in Nigeria during the
Biafran War. He was Superior of the Anglo-Irish Province of the
Vincentian Community in 1980. He has also worked in parish
ministry serving in Dunstable in England and in Harryville,
Ballymena during the recent 'happenings' there. At present he is
working in St John's Parish, Belfast.

THE FOLLOWING THREE QUOTATIONS INTRIGUE ME. FIRST, "THE Unionist Party, by the manner in which they have approved and preached doctrines of violence and lawlessness have, I say, disqualified themselves forever. The flame of Irish Nationalism is inextinguishable." Not the vapourings of a latter day Republican extremist, but the words of Winston Churchill in Belfast in 1912.

The next is from the late Enoch Powell. On being asked in an interview how often he went to Ireland, he replied coldly that he "never went to Ireland, but frequently to Ulster..." Even though Ulster is one of Ireland's four provinces.

Finally, "I regard myself as an Ulster man first, British second and finally - in a strictly geographical sense - Irish"! This last from Ian Major, a contributor to ECONI's earlier book *Faith in Ulster*. Could this be taken as a definition of a Unionist?

Ulster, Irish, Loyalist, Unionist, Nationalist? We could do with a little clarification here! No wonder the ancients insisted on the aphorism *initium disputandi definitio nominis* as a prerequisite for any meaningful dialogue - before you begin, say clearly what you mean by the terms you use.

In our present impasse it seems almost impossible to do that. How does one define Unionism? Ken Maginnis, in an article written in 1986, appreciated the problem when he wrote, "Unionists are not, though often portrayed as such, a humourless, intransigent and almost monolithic Protestant grouping."

If you threw in the epithets 'fearful' and 'suspicious' it would probably, I have to say, represent many an outsider's view of Unionists - though that is to caricature, not to define. Like many another political party or group, Unionism has its moderates, liberals, hard-liners and extremists.

Terence O'Neill and others showed that it was possible for Unionists to edge forward from entrenched positions. I believe the finest hour for moderate Unionism came with the Power Sharing Executive in 1973-1974. Enormous credit is due to Brian Faulkner for showing that it was possible, after all, for Unionists and Nationalists to work together for the good of Northern Ireland.

I believe that the significance of the overthrow of the Executive as a result of the workers strike can hardly be exaggerated. I have seen this strike described, incredibly, as the 'Constitutionalist Stoppage'! What is being referred to is the week when Northern Ireland witnessed high treason in the streets - and saw it succeed. Paramilitarism and naked terror overthrew legitimate government. Moderate Unionism's courageous stand, exemplified by Brian Faulkner, was finally betrayed.

The process that led to the creation of the Executive in 1974 was a process in which mutual respect came to grow and develop. We need to recreate that process and that mutual respect today.

Paul
O'CONNOR

Paul O' Connor was born and raised in Derry. He has worked as a co-ordinator at the Derry based Pat Finucane Centre since the group was formed in 1992. The Centre organises the annual Bloody Sunday commemoration in Derry. It is also active in promoting debate around issues including policing, human rights and engagement between unionists and nationalists. Named in memory of the murdered Belfast solicitor Pat Finucane, the Centre has published a number of reports and maintains an archive on various aspects of the conflict. The group promotes a non-violent ethos and is not aligned to any political party.

LANDLORDS, OLD MEN, HYPHENATED SURNAMES, PROTESTANT, TIGHT, tough, stubborn, powerful, red white n' blue, groundrents, faceless, O'Neillites, Paisleyites, liberal, conservative, Sirs and Lords, Ulstermen, dour, B specials, Londonderry, gerrymander, district inspectors, old men, presbyterian, hard working, boring, serious, bigoted, RUC men, Sundays n' swings, head for the border, cannae sing and aren't allowed, cannae dance neither, orangees, the Fountain and prods, Lundy burning, Apprentice Boys, old men, Harland and Wolffe, sectarianism, job-lodge-job, us n' them, them n' us, The Bible! and before I forget...just to rub it in...no bloody sense of humour.

Growing up in Derry in the sixties that was fairly much it in a nutshell - my understanding of unionism, or to be more precise, unionists. At the time unionism and Protestantism was as natural a linkage as the Pope and Rome.

The only real unionist I knew owned the property we lived in. In fact he owned the whole street - and still does. And he did seem an 'old man'. He had a moustache and had been an officer in the British Army. That was a generation ago. We have all moved on since '68 - excepting of course the generations who were buried in the process.

Gregory Campbell has reminded us that a unionist working class exists, and always did. Though sharp wits counter the 'we-too-had-coal-in-the-bath' claim with the outrageous suggestion that *they* at least had coal. Even the 'Big Man' from Ballymena has softened. David Trimble has shown courageous leadership and the modernisers are slowly winning out over the traditionalists within unionism. Anti-Catholicism, or at the very least, non-Catholicism, is no longer a defining feature of unionist ideology. The majority of unionists have voluntarily entered a process involving compromise and respect for the first time since Ulster unionism emerged as an ideology in the last decades of the nineteenth century. Time to reassess before the community relations police come calling. That's the theory at least.

Nothing is quite so simple any more. I don't equate unionism with 'protest'antism. That powerful protesting, questioning and rebellious tradition within European Protestantism is no longer recognisable in the North of Ireland. 1798 and all that. The historical, and in particular, the demographic realities of the settler/native relationship on this island put paid to any anti-authoritarian notion of nailing a thesis on the door. Guarding the door from within took precedence.

Defence of the State, a role which no church should undertake, has characterised Ulster Protestantism, particularly since 1922. My country right or wrong. The most obvious manifestation of this is the continuing unholy alliance between Ulster unionism, Orangeism and the Protestant churches.

Over sixty Officers of the Grand Orange Lodge of Ireland are ministers of religion, for example. The Order in turn has official delegate status on the Ulster Unionist Council. The largest political party within the unionist family continues to define itself in clearly sectarian terms.

Anti-Catholicism, or at the very least, non-Catholicism, remains, sadly, a defining feature of unionist ideology. The unionist family, dysfunctional though it may be in recent times, remains essentially united - for all the wrong reasons. United through fear and a perception of threat (which the IRA campaign undoubtedly confirmed), united in opposition to something, and by default.

The motivation for that unity is not positive. It didn't evolve out of a shared sense of values and community, but rather out of a fear of the other community and the need for self-preservation and protection. It may seem like heresy to say this in the fluffy feel-good atmosphere that has dominated official discourse since the signing of the Agreement, but I remain to be convinced that anti-Catholicism is no longer the defining feature of unionism.

Before explaining why, I should first come clean and admit that the very nature of the modernising 'yes' versus traditionalist 'no' debate within unionism gives cause for concern.

I don't actually believe that the Big Man from Ballymena has softened, that David Trimble has shown courageous leadership, or that the majority of unionists have voluntarily entered a process involving compromise and respect. I do believe that the two governments devised an extremely clever set of circumstances which made it virtually impossible for anyone to withdraw at the last moment. Unionists were cajoled, most unwillingly, into the latter half of the twentieth century.

But back to the internal debate. Ambiguity best describes the reaction of many observing the daily duels on our television screens between the unionist 'yes' and 'no' camps. It didn't really matter who landed the most devastating low blow since it was unionist on unionist. Spectator sport for non-unionists. But many people commented at the time, "If this is how unionist politicians treat each other how will they treat us?" The debates were aggressive, insulting, lacking in respect, and fundamentally male. The purpose was to savage, humiliate and verbally maul the opponent.

I recall a delegate emerging flustered from a meeting in Jeffrey Donaldson's constituency. He was devastated by the experience, as he admitted to a waiting television camera. The question is valid: If this characterises relationships within the unionist family, exactly how deep is the well of respect and tolerance for those on the outside?

That brings us back to sectarianism. At a recent event I asked a unionist whom I would regard as someone I could do business with why he had joined the Orange Order. The person in question is regarded as one of the up and coming young bloods within the Unionist Party. A 'liberal'.

In my naiveté I expected a response along the lines of lodge equals status equals party career. Instead, he explained his interpretation and understanding of the Old Testament and, by definition, his acceptance of the Orange Order oath which pledges to "strenuously oppose the fatal errors and doctrines of the Church of Rome." I was dumbfounded.

Asked if he could see his way to entering a Catholic chapel to attend the wedding of a friend, he replied that he couldn't, ever. It was an honest, even relaxed, discussion. But it left me profoundly depressed and perplexed in equal measure. A world view was explained to me that was outside all intellectual reference points.

I expressed the opinion that, taken to its most extreme, this was the ultimate justification for those who would take the life of another human being merely because the victim belonged to the Church of Rome. Most unionists, and certainly the individual concerned, have been appalled by sectarian murders.

The real contradiction, however, is that sectarianism, opposition to Roman Catholicism, is the cement which has held unionism together. For a minority, this fixation on Rome is based on bizarre interpretations of the Bible. For the majority, sectarianism has been a matter of political expediency, a mechanism which created an artificial sense of ethnic bonding, helped to maintain power and justified the unjustifiable.

There are of course a prophetic minority who dissent and argue that unionism should not be aligned with Protestantism. As we approach the end of the millennium, it remains to be seen which direction unionism will ultimately take.

Gerry REYNOLDS

Gerry Reynolds CSsR belongs to the Roman Catholic religious order known as Redemptorists. A native of Mungret, County Limerick, he joined the Redemptorists in 1953 and was ordained a priest in 1960. He has been a member of the Redemptorist community at Clonard Monastery since 1983. He is involved in the peace and reconciliation ministry of Clonard Monastery. As part of that ministry he is a member of Cornerstone Community - an inter-church group which works for reconciliation in the Shankill/Falls interface in West Belfast. Together with Rev Ken Newell, minister of Fitzroy Presbyterian Church, he has helped to build up the Clonard / Fitzroy Fellowship. The members of this fellowship contribute to the growth of mutual understanding between the two traditions and have developed a sense of shared responsibility for the well-being of the whole community.

THE MAKING OF A MIRACLE

ONE OF THE FIRST PROTESTANTS I MET AFTER COMING TO LIVE IN Belfast in 1983 was Dr George Dallas who died in 1997. He saw himself in the tradition of his fellow Presbyterian, Rev J.B. Armour of Ballymoney. An original thinker and courageous Christian man, his sense of the Protestant community in Ireland fascinated me. I quote from what he wrote in *The Furrow:*

Our sense of Britishness dates mainly from the Victorian era, which saw a profound emotional tie-up between evangelical Protestantism, the Royal Family and the British Empire, with whose growing power and prestige people felt proud to be associated. In the eighteenth century we had been Irish, albeit Protestant Irish.

We hated England, but continued to serve her because our fear of the Catholics and contempt for them over-ruled even our own interest. Sooner or later we will be forced to look at the truth that not only have we never been British, but all along, whether we like it or not, we have been Irish.

The murals of the Shankill state in stark relief that the Protestant people of Northern Ireland do not see themselves as Irish now. And the Peace Line wall of separation between Clonard Monastery, where I live, and the Shankill stands on alienating foundations deep in their sub-conscious. I have found that George Mitchell's portrait of the people on each side of the wall is very accurate, "To the outsider both are warm and generous. Between themselves they are fearful and antagonistic." But I have also found that the lived human reality is far more complex than what the wall and murals signify.

Ordinary people of the Falls will tell you that they have more in common with the Shankill people than with the people of southern Ireland. An elderly woman, a retired music teacher, said to me recently, "I identify better with the Protestants of Belfast than with the Catholics of the South - even though my mother and father were from the Republic." What does that say about the primary identity of both the Shankill people and the Falls people? There is a profound common bond. I am certain an immense creative energy will flow from that bond as soon as genuine dialogue makes both sides conscious of it together.

I remember a local woman, now dead, who was about to pray one day in Clonard saying to me, "I'm going to sit in the church now and look at God." I asked her, "Will you look at him with all the people of Belfast, Catholic and Protestant, Falls and Shankill in your heart?" "Sure I will, for aren't we the same? And isn't each of us precious in his eyes?" Such convictions are part of that common bond that is deeper than the evident alienation. This light shines in the darkness!

In my early days in Belfast, I would often look from the monastery window towards the Shankill. A verse from Psalm 42 came to embody my feeling towards the people who lived there, "When can I enter and see the face of God?"

Years later, I was sitting in a Shankill kitchen drinking tea with a woman whose son had been killed a few months earlier by the IRA. The terrible tragedy and pain of his death was very present to us as we chatted away about everyday things. Then the chat stopped. She looked at me and said ever so simply and gently, "If only they had known him, they could never have killed him." That is, known him in his full and mysterious identity as a human person, known him as the child she bore with the unique love of a mother. Her murdered son was for that mother the face of God. Do you think any bereaved mother is any different from her in this?

We find God's presence where the dialogue is. Dialogue is the name of our God. The absence of dialogue is the absence of God and the breeding ground of all sorts of alienation and demonisation. Those who see no point in dialogue are in reality putting themselves in a Godless and hopeless situation.

I once asked the boys in the senior class of St Gall's primary school, beside Clonard Monastery what we could propose to people on the Shankill side of the Wall that would improve relationships. At the end of many suggestions a boy who had been silent said, "Ask them to say yes to us." We will come to know our complex identity better when we say 'yes' to one another as contemporary human beings who share this little part of the fertile earth. And coming to know one another in friendship will open people up to discovering new dimensions of their identity.

I am convinced that through their 'yes' to us, Unionist people will come to be at ease with themselves, not only as part of the British-Irish family of peoples, but also as part of the family of peoples who share the island of Ireland. And through the same process I believe that Republican people will come to realise that the freedom to be ourselves and the union of the people of Britain and Ireland do not stand in contradiction to one another. They are complementary values. A settlement that is fair to all must reflect both.

Pray each day with me for your part and mine in the making of this miracle, "Lord help us to grow to-day in mutual understanding and to work for a settlement that is fair to all."

Geraldine SMYTH

Geraldine Smyth is a Dominican theologian. A native of Belfast, she has a background in education, psychotherapy and theology, and sees herself as a 'crosser of borders', committed to correlating theology with social, political and cultural issues. A graduate of the University of Ulster, she also holds a PhD in theology from Trinity College, Dublin. She is director of the Irish School of Ecumenics, whose research on Moving Beyond Sectarianism and educational programmes for peace and reconciliation in Northern Ireland, the Republic of Ireland and beyond seek to deepen mutual respect and understanding among people of different cultures and church traditions.

I N THESE POST-MODERN DAYS WHEN EVERY 'ISM' AND GRAND SCHEME falls suspect, even the most steadfast political monoliths are seen to overlap and reinvent themselves. Unionism is no exception, and one must acknowledge the diversity within the unionist family. Until recently, however, differentiation tended to take the form of more reactionary splinter groups of deeper dye. There are signs of a new self-questioning, creative diversity, but before acknowledging these, I offer an impressionistic outsider's view of 'traditional' unionism. Given the imposed brevity, generalization and some type-casting are inevitable, but I will endeavour to avoid stereotyping.

Over the years, unionism looked to the past. Its recurring slogans were *Remember!* or *No surrender!* - its emotional energy playing between nostalgia and a determination to hold the status quo. Its symbolic universe featured walls, painted boundary-markers and mythologized battles. Often in step with the Loyal Orders, its internal preoccupation was the necessity of unbroken ranks. Unionist supremacy imposed itself civically in the architecture of the City Hall, Stormont and local Orange Halls. Unionist success seemed to rest on the Protestant work ethic and positions of privilege in shipyard and linen mill, Civil Service and Farmers' Association.

Moving cyclically within a closed system, unionism strove to maintain or recover some original state of 'civil and religious liberty'. How that vision could be expressed here and now did not really matter. Historic events such as the Siege of Derry were ritualized annually as the 'chosen trauma'. Commemoration of 'innocent settlers' besieged by 'treacherous natives' bred a siege mentality, sustaining the twin tendency of looking to Britain for rescue, and a distrust of Catholic or Gael.

Thus, a boundary separated the innocent from the betrayer. Unionist innocence was a permanent assumption, with the equal presumption that the 'other side' could not be trusted. Notwithstanding neighbourly civility, suspicion was a requirement, compounded by conspiracy theories of Rome-rule lurking inside the Trojan horse of nationalism and the never far away nationalist stab in the back.

Hence the unionist emphasis on vigilance and security, law and order. There must be no dereliction of duty to itself, no compromise with woolly liberalism. Was it then a fear of self-destruction, of sawing off the branch it sits on, rather than a will to dominate that made the prospect of sharing power - until recently - unthinkable for unionists?

One noted author speaks of the pattern of Ulster history in terms of 'the narrow ground', suggesting a reductionist approach to politics and fixation on the single issue of 'the Union'. In this context, dialogue spelled sell-out, inclusiveness equalled absorption into a United Ireland, and ecumenism was a euphemism for the watering down of denominational heritage and particularity.

The rhetoric of unionism has played on images of 'scarcity' and its first cousins, purity and purism, promoting a self-understanding of the chosen few living by the straight and narrow, against the day when accounts must be strictly settled, ever undeceived by the blandishments of the Celtic imagination.

Allowing for variations, unionism reflects aspects of Protestant churches' polity, particularly the capacity for broad participation and the key role of individual conscience. The complex system of checks and balances, at its best, ensures a voice for all concerned, but sometimes leaves no room for manoeuvre when a situation calls for accommodation, or when rigid adherence to legal principle may force a rift. Interlocking processes of decision-making set limits on power that would impose itself collectively or from above.

Protestant preference for simplicity of worship - for word over image - is mirrored in a demand for clear ideas couched in no-nonsense language, shorn of verbal ambiguity. But, the pared-down approach of Ulster Protestantism has often adopted the negative side of the prophetic principle - protesting against - rather than the positive tradition of protesting for. Not without basis, Catholic nationalists have viewed Protestantism as unionism at prayer, as a covenant of throne and pulpit that functioned to exclude them.

The penchant for plain speaking has sometimes resulted in 'literal' applications of Biblical texts on providence, covenant and land, to legitimize abuses of political power (not much different from nationalism's appropriation of symbols of Christ's death and resurrection as a religious canopy over a politics of victimhood and violent uprising). Confessional dogmas of who is 'saved' were invoked to uphold a sectarian politics of *For God and Ulster*. Paradoxically, the Calvinist doctrine of the sovereignty of God could be linked, in one zealous move, to the unquestioned sovereignty of state and parliament.

Perhaps a contemporary Protestant retrieval of the doctrine of justification by grace through faith, or fresh reflection on Paul's God-given insight - "My grace is sufficient for thee" - will spill over into unionism and beyond, encouraging a trust in the reality that beyond all our futile claims to innocence lies the fragile hope of a fresh start, a move from the "logic of equivalence" to the "logic of redemption" (Paul Ricoeur). Beyond the illusion of scarcity, God knows what sources of generosity may yet flow freely.

There never was a golden age of innocence - in the seventeenth century or at any other time. No-one has clean hands. None can claim a monopoly of hurt. Victims and victimizers co-exist inside every person and party. There is no innocent place to start. We are powerless to secure our identities in isolation. We need one another in our differences for the sake of relationship and for the sake of truth.

I welcome the emergence of the new unionist parties growing out from paramilitary organizations, as a bold community-based contribution to a unionist politics beyond sectarian or class exclusions.

I welcome the emerging visibility of the female face of unionism, and am impressed by some unionists' capacity for re-thinking unionism and their confident articulation of an alternative unionist vision.

I salute the imagination and risk-taking by the current unionist leadership in moving towards the realization of 'a pluralist parliament for a pluralist people.'

We live in interesting times. Questions remain: Can the Stormont Agreement and new political structures become the opportunity for unionist and nationalist politics to be genuinely transformed? Will unionists and nationalists honestly engage each other - and engage those who subscribe to neither establishment - in robust dialogue and mutual critique? Is co-operation possible on issues of social, economic and ecological concern? How can we, together, forge a political culture of interdependence adequate to the next millennium?